EAST INDIANS IN THE CARIBBEAN

Frontispiece Poem

THEY CAME IN SHIPS

They came in ships
From across the seas, they came
Britain, colonising India, transporting her chains
From Chota agpur and the Ganges plains.

Westwards came the Whitby,
The Hesperus
The Island-bound Fatel Rozack

Wooden missions of imperialist design
Human victims of her Majesty's victory

They came in fleets
They came in droves
Like cattle
Brown like cattle
Eyes limpid, like cattle

Some came with dreams of milk and honey riches
Fleeing famine and death:
Dancing girls
Rajput soldiers, determined, tall
Escaping penalty of pride
Stolen wives, afraid and despondent,
Crossing black waters,
Brahmin, Chammar, alike
Hearts brimful of hope

-Mahadai Das (Guyana)

EAST INDIANS IN THE CARIBBEAN

AN ILLUSTRATED HISTORY

Florence Pariag

ARAWAK
publications
Kingston Jamaica

A r a w a k publications
17 Kensington Crescent
Kingston 5

Printed in Singapore

976 8189 05 3

NATIONAL LIBRARY OF JAMAICA CATALOGUING IN PUBLICATION DATA

Pariag, Florence
East Indians in the Caribbean : an illustrated
history / Florence Pariag

p. : ill. ; cm.. – (Caribbean ethnic studies)
Includes bibliographical references and index

ISBN 976-8189-05-3

1. East Indians – West Indies. 2. East Indians – Trinidad.
3. East Indians – Jamaica. 4. East Indians – Guyana.
5. Immigrants – West Indies. I. Title

305.8914110729 - dc.20

Cover picture: "Coolie Colours" by Bernadette Persaud (Guyana)

Illustrations (line drawings): Kojovi Dawes

Photographs: Courtesy of the National Library of Jamaica; the Library, University of the West Indies, Mona, Jamaica; the Library, University of the West Indies, St Augustine, Trinidad dedicated to

John Kenrick Pariag

and to

Bhagirath and Sumintra Ramharry

for their example of discipline and hard work

Contents

List of Illustrations

Acknowledgements

I would like to thank Dr. Brinsley Samaroo of the University of the West Indies, St. Augustine, Trinidad, and Professor Verene Shepherd of the University of the West Indies, Mona, Jamaica for their critical comments and constructive advice on the draft of this publication.

I also thank my colleagues at the Library, University of the West Indies, Mona, in particular, Margarette Pearce and Gracelyn Cassell, for their encouragement and support. I am grateful to Bernadette Persaud and Gwyneth George of Guyana, and Laura Hosein and family of Trinidad, who helped in acquiring special materials for this book.

Finally, I thank my children, David, Rachael and Joel, who helped in many intangible ways.

Abolition and Indenture

Chapter 1

What were our origins?

Who were our **ancestors**?

How did we arrive at this point, or this **crossroads** in history?

(Bedaridé 17)

East Indians came to the Caribbean as indentured labourers to work on the sugar plantations. An indenture is a contract by which a person is bound to serve or work for someone else for a specified period. The system of indentured labour was used in the seventeenth century by the planters in the Caribbean. They needed labour to clear the land and start production of crops and they recruited white indentured labourers from the United Kingdom.

In *White Servitude and Black Slavery in Barbados 1627-1715*, Beckles states:

> "*It was common practice in seventeenth century England for farmers to hire servants by the year for agricultural and artisan work. The logical next step, therefore, was to demand labour from England under temporary indenture, not for a year but for between three and ten years. Masters would pay passages and feed, clothe, and shelter servants in return for their labour. At the end of indenture, in a practice consistent with the labour culture of the Stuart society, the servant would receive a 'freedom due' of ten pounds or a piece of land.*"
>
> (Beckles 3)

Indians in Uganda building the railway.These labourers were part of the Indian diaspora.

This system of labour declined during slavery, but was used again in the nineteenth century when there was a demand by planters for cheap labour.

After the abolition of slavery in 1834, the freed slaves settled in their own villages, or found employment in towns. The sugar planters in the Caribbean faced bankruptcy without a cheap source of labour on the plantations. They requested the Colonial Office in Great Britain to set up a system to recruit labourers from India, China and Portugal. However, there was opposition to the system of indentured labour.

In 1840, Lord John Russell, the British Secretary of State, made the following statement concerning the export of labourers from India to British Guiana:

> *"I should be unwilling to adopt any measure to favour the transfer of labourers from India to British Guiana . . . I am not prepared to encounter the responsibility of a measure which may lead to dreadful loss of life on one hand, or on the other hand to a new system of slavery."*
>
> -Tinker (see Frontispiece)

The East Indians were the largest group of indentured labourers, who came to the Caribbean. From 1838 to 1918, approximately 429,000 East Indians arrived to work on the sugar plantations. Most of them went to Guiana, Trinidad and Suriname, and smaller numbers went to Jamaica, Grenada, Martinique and Guadeloupe.

The Indian Diaspora

East Indians also went as labourers to other countries such as Mauritius, Fiji, Burma and South Africa. There are East Indian communities in these countries today, and these communities are similar in many ways. This dispersal of people is called the Indian diaspora.

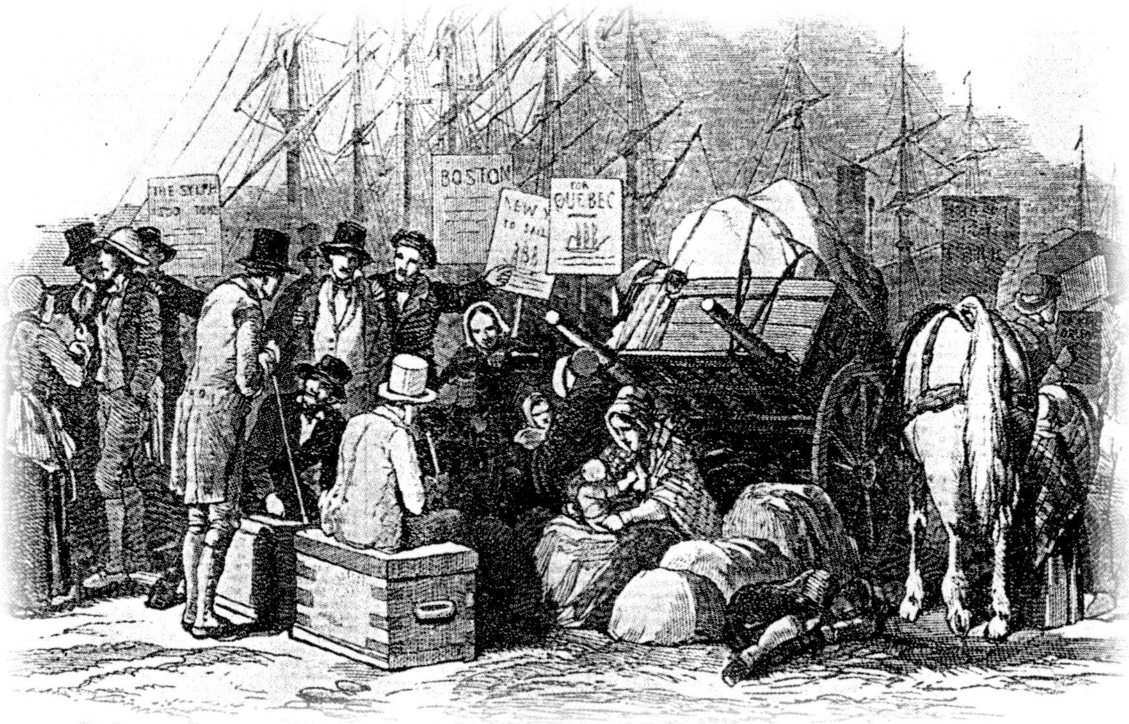

Emigrants at Cork, Ireland, waiting to sail to the United States, 19th century

Two Migrations

This movement of people from India in the nineteenth century was part of a larger worldwide migration, of people crossing the oceans in search of new opportunities. Europeans travelled across the Atlantic to the Americas. Asians, from India and China, migrated to plantations in tropical countries and they provided labour to produce sugar, tea and cocoa for the world market. In the Caribbean, they provided the labour to cut and grind the sugar cane. During these 100 years, about one hundred million persons from Europe and Asia crossed the oceans in search of new opportunities.

Sidney Mintz writes that both groups of migrants resulted in second generations that included physicians, novelists and politicians. But one did so under social and economic conditions that facilitated considerable upward mobility. The other did so under social and economic conditions that guaranteed, above all, the commodity harvests of sugar and coffee for the world market, and in which social and economic opportunity were severely restricted. *(Look Lai xxviii)*

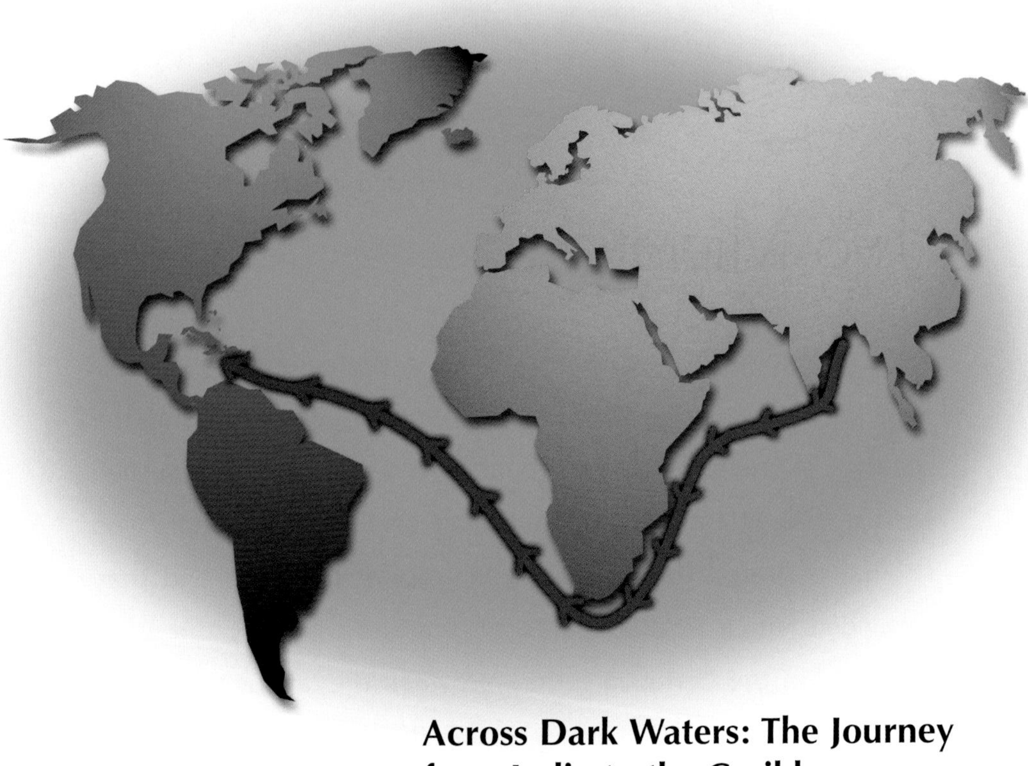

Across Dark Waters: The Journey from India to the Caribbean

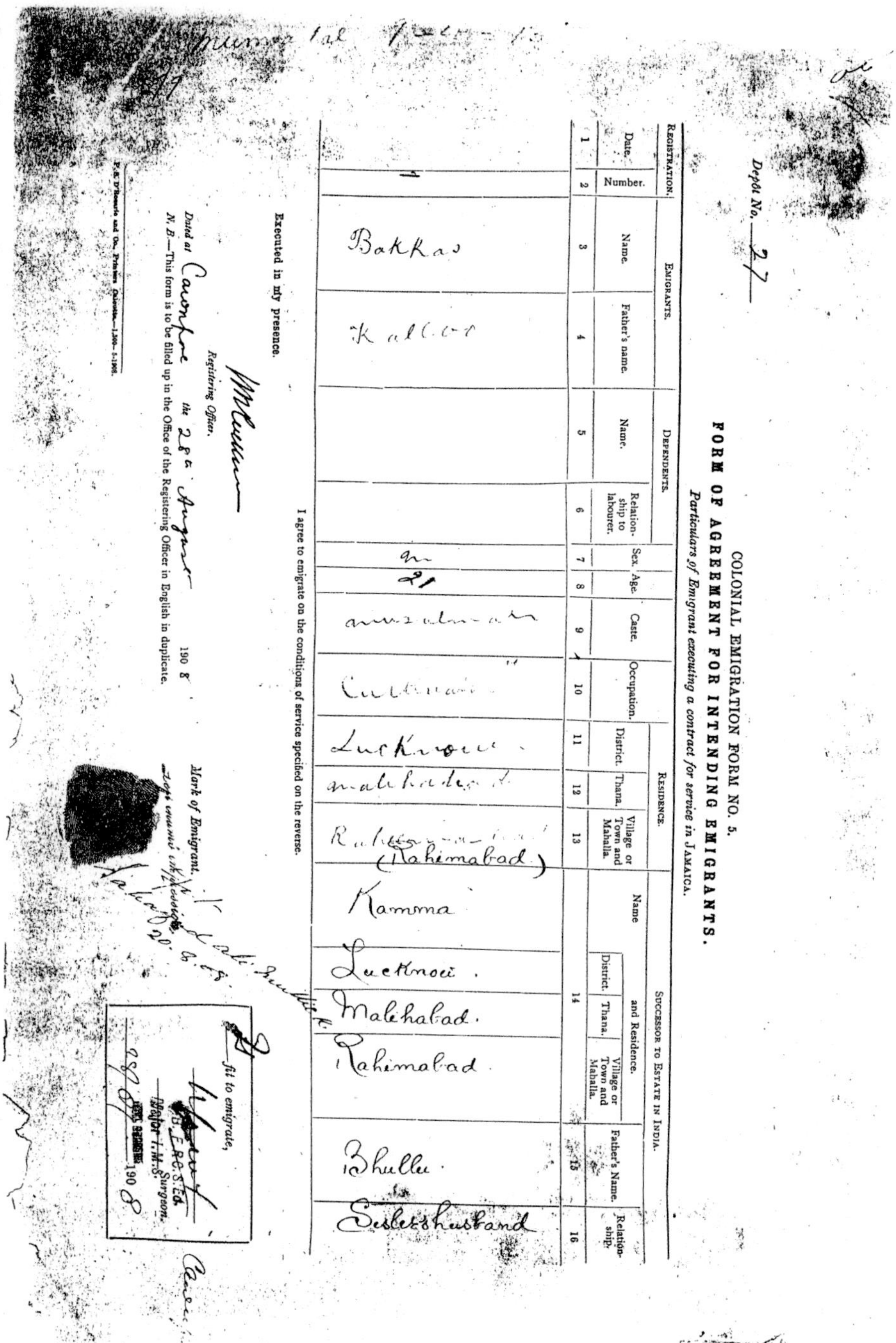

Depôt No. 27

COLONIAL EMIGRATION FORM NO. 5.

FORM OF AGREEMENT FOR INTENDING EMIGRANTS.

Particulars of Emigrant executing a contract for service in JAMAICA.

Registration.		Emigrants.		Dependents.						Residence.			Successor to Estate in India.					
Date.	Number.	Name.	Father's name.	Name.	Relationship to labourer.	Sex.	Age.	Caste.	Occupation.	District.	Thana.	Village or Town and Mahalla.	Name and Residence.	District.	Thana.	Village or Town and Mahalla.	Father's Name.	Relationship.
1	2	3	4	5	6	7	8	9	10	11	12	13	14				15	16
	1	Bakkas	Kallor			m	21	musalman	Cultivator	Lucknow	malihabad	Rahimabad (Rahimabad)	Kamma	Lucknow.	Malihabad.	Rahimabad.	Bhullu.	Sister's husband

I agree to emigrate on the conditions of service specified on the reverse.

Executed in my presence.

Registering Officer.

Dated at Cawnpore the 28th August 1908

N. B.—This form is to be filled up in the Office of the Registering Officer in English in duplicate.

Mark of Emigrant.

fit to emigrate,

F.R.C.S.Ed.
Surgeon.
Major I.M.S.

1908

F. K. D'Rozario and Co., Printers Calcutta.—1,500—5-1908.

Contract of Indenture

JAMAICA.

Conditions of Service and Terms of Agreement which the Recruiter is Authorized to offer on behalf of the Agent to Intending Emigrants.

Period of Service. Five years from date of arrival in the Colony.

Nature of Labour. Work in connection with the cultivation of the soil or the manufacture of the produce on any plantation and domestic service.

Number of days on which the Emigrant is required to labour in each week. Every day, excepting Sundays and authorized holidays.

Number of hours in each day during which he is required to labour without extra remuneration Nine hours.

Monthly or daily wages or task work rates. When employed at time-work every adult male Emigrant above the age of sixteen years will be paid not less than one shilling, which is at present equivalent to twelve annas, and every adult female Emigrant above the age of twelve years and every male Emigrant of any age between twelve and sixteen years not less than nine pence, which is at present equivalent to nine annas, for every working day of nine hours; children below these ages will receive wages proportionate to the amount of work done.

Any adult Emigrant may be permitted to do Task or Ticca work, and when so employed, after the Emigrant has had practice and experience, he may earn much more than one shilling a day.

Wages are paid weekly.

Conditions as to return passage. Emigrants on completing a continuous residence of ten years in Jamaica and having during that time obtained or become entitled to a Certificate of Industrial Service, shall be entitled to be provided at the expense of the Colony with a passage back to Calcutta, on payment in the case of a man of one-half of the passage money, and in the case of a woman, of one-third of such passage money. The Children, dependents or wives of such Emigrants to receive a free passage provided they accompany such Emigrant.

Provided that such Emigrants as are destitute or disabled shall, with children, dependents or wives, be entitled to a free return passage. Persons who have previously proceeded to the Colony and returned to India shall not be entitled to return passages. After completing a continuous residence of five years, and holding or becoming entitled to a Certificate of Industrial Service, Emigrants may return to India at their own cost. Blankets and warm clothing are supplied gratis on leaving India, but not for the return voyage.

Every Emigrant, however, who at any time quits the Colony, shall thereby forfeit all claim to an assisted return passage at the expense of the Colony though he or she may have resided ten years in the Colony.

Other conditions. Emigrants will receive rations from their employers during the first three months after their arrival in the Colony according to the scale prescribed by the Government of Jamaica, at a weekly cost of two shillings and six pence, which is at present equivalent to one rupee and fourteen annas, for each person of twelve years of age and upwards.

Each child between one and twelve years of age will receive half rations at a weekly cost of one shilling and three pence, which is at present equivalent to fifteen annas.

Suitable dwellings will be assigned to Emigrants under indenture free of rent and will be kept in good repair by the employers. When Emigrants under indenture are ill they will be provided with Hospital accommodation, Medical attendance, Medicines, Medical Comforts and Food free of charge.

नोकरी का समय—कालोनी या टापु में पहुंचने की तारीख से पांच बरस ।

काम का तौर—वह काम जो ज़मीन के जोतने या खेत के उपजे अन्न को कारीगरी में लाने और घर के काम काज से लगाव रखता हो ।

परदेशी कुलीयों को जितने दिन हर हफ़ते में काम करने पड़ेगा—इतवार और ठहराई हुई छुट्टी के दिनों को छोड़ के सब दिन ।

बिन ऊपरी मज़दूरी के हर दिन में जितने घण्टे परदेशी कुली को काम करना पड़ेगा—हर दिन में नौ घण्टे काम करना पड़ेगा ।

महीनावारी या रोज़रोज़ की मज़दूरी या ठीके काम का दर—जब रोज़ का काम मिलेगा हर एक भला चंगा मरद परदेशी कुली को जिसकी उमर सोलह बरस से ऊपर है एक शिलिंग जो कि आजकाल बारह आने के बराबर है मिलेगा और हर एक जवान औरत परदेशी कुली को जिसकी उमर बारह बरस से ऊपर है और हर एक मरद परदेशी कुली को जिसकी उमर बारह और सोलह बरस के भीतर है नौ पेन्स जो कि आजकाल नौ आने के बराबर है ऐसे नौ घण्टे काम करने के हर एक दिन के लिये मिलेगा और लड़के या लड़कियां जिनकी उमर इन उमरों से कम है जितना काम करेंगे उतना ही मज़दूरी पावेंगे ।

जवान परदेशी कुली को चुकती का या ठीका का काम जो अपनी और मालिक की खुशी से लेगा मिलेगा और जब उसको इस तरह का काम मिले और परदेशी कुली काम को अच्छा तरह समझ लेवे और काम से वाकिफ़ हो जावे तब हर एक दिन एक शिलिंग से और भी ज़ियादे कमा सकेगा ।

अठवारे अठवारे तलब दी जाती है ।

लौट आने की शरतें—अगर परदेशी कुली जमैका टापु में दस बरस बराबर रहकर मेहनत का काम की सार्टिफ़िकेट पावे या पाने के हक़दार होवे तो वह कुली हर एक मरद के लिये राह-खरच का आधा और औरत के लिये तीन हिस्सा का एक हिस्सा राह खरच दाखिल करने से टापू की तरफ़ से कलकत्ते तक पहुंचा दिया जायेगा । ऐसे कुली के लड़केवाले और जोरू और घराने अगर उसके साथ आवें तो बिना खरच आने सकेंगे ।

पर जो कुली लाचार और बहुत गरीब हो वह लड़के बालों को और जोरू और अपने घराने के लोगों को साथ लेकर बिना खरच लौट आने सकेगा । जो कुली एकबार टापु में से होकर हिन्दुस्तान आया था वह फिर लौट आने का खरच नहीं पावेगा । लगातार पांच बरस रहकर अगर कोई कुली मेहनत का काम करने के लिये सर्टिफ़िकेट पावे या पाने का हक़दार होवे तो अपने खरच से हिन्दुस्तान में लौट आने सकता है । जाने का वक़त कम्मल और गरम कपड़ा मुफ़त दिया जाता पर आने का समय नहीं ।

अगर कोई कुली कोई समय टापु छोड़ दिया हो तो वह हिन्दुस्तान में लौट आने वकत टापु की तरफ़ से कुछ मदद नहीं पावेगा चाहे वह टापु में पुरा दस बरस रहा हो कि नहीं ।

दूसरी शरतें—कालानी या टापु में पहुंचने के पीछे हर एक परदेशी कुली को उसके मालीक की ओर से खाना जमैका गवरन्मेण्ट के ठहराए हुए हिसाब से पहिले तीन महीने भर हर हफ़ता दो शिलिंग छः पेन्स जो कि आजकाल एक रुपया चौदा आने के बराबर है देने से हर एक को जिसकी उमर बारह बरस या ज़ियादे है मिलेगा ।

हर एक लड़के या लड़की को जिसका उमर एक और बारह बरस के भीतर है एक शिलिंग तीन पेन्स जो कि आजकाल पंद्रह आनेका बराबर है देने से बड़ों का आधा खाना मिलेगा ।

परदेशी कुलीयों को इक़रार नामे के मुवाफ़िक़ रहने के लायक घर बे किराए के मिलेगा जिसकी मरमत मालिक की ओर से अच्छी तरह होगी ।

और जब परदेशी कुली लोग जो इक़रार नाम के मुवाफ़िक़ हैं बीमार पड़ेंगे उन को अस्पताल में जगह मिलेगी और डाक्टर दवाई बीमार-योग्य खाना और मामूली खाना बिन दाम के मिलेगा ।

نوکري کي ميعاد — کالوني يا ٹاپو مين پہنچنے کي تاريخ سے پانچ برس -

مزدوري کي قسم — وہ کام جو زمين کے جوتنے يا کاشت کي پيداوار کو کاريگري مين لائي اور گھر کے کام سے لگاو رکھتا ہو -

جتنے دن ہر ہفتہ مين پرديسي قليون کو کام کرنا ہوگا — اتوار اور مقرري چھٹي کے دنون کو چھوڑ کے سب دن -

ہر دن جتنے گھنٹے پرديسي قليون کو بلا اوپري مزدوري کے کام کرنا ہوگا — ہر دن مين نو گھنٹے کام کرنا ہوگا -

ماہواري يا روز روز کي مزدوري يا چکتي کام کا در — جب گھنٹے کے حساب کام مليگا ہر ايک جوان مرد پرديسي قلي کو جسکي عمر سولہ برس سے زيادہ ہي ايک شلنگ جو کہ آج کل بارہ آنے کے برابر ہی مليگا اور ہر ايک جوان عورت پرديسي قلي کو جسکي عمر بارہ برس سے زيادہ ہی اور ہر ايک مرد پرديسي قلي جسکي عمر بارہ اور سولہ برس کے اندر ہی نو پنس جو کہ آج کل نو آنے کے برابر ہی ايسے نو گھنٹے کام کرنے کے ہر ايک دن کے ليئے مليگا اور لڑکے يا لڑکيان جنکي عمر اُن لکھی ہوئے عمرون سے کم ہی جتنا کام کرينگے اُتناہي مزدوري پاوينگے -

جوان پرديسي قلي کو چکتي يا ٹھيکہ کام جو اپنے اور مالک کي خوشي سے ليگا مليگا اور جب اوسکو اسطرحکا کام مليگا اور وہ پرديسي قلي اچھي طرح کام کرنے لگيگا اور کام سے واقف ہو جاويگا تب ہر ايک دن مين ايک شلنگ سے اور بھي زيادہ کما سکيگا -

طلب ہفتے ہفتے دي جاتي ہی -

لوٹ آنے کي شرطين — اگر پرديسي قلي جميکا ٹاپو مين دس برس برابر رہکر محنت کے کام کي سرٹيفيکٹ پاوے يا پانے کے حقدار ہووے تو وہ مرد ہو تو راہ خرچ کا آدھا اور عورت ہو تو راہ خرچ کا تين حصہ کا ايک حصہ داخل کردينے سے ٹاپو کي طرف سے ہندوستان مين پہونچا ديا جاويگا - اور اوس کے لڑکے اور جورو اور اوس کے گھرانے اگر اوسکے ساتھ آوے تو بلا خرچ ہندوستان مين آنے پاوينگے -

پر جو قلي لاچار اور بہت غريب ہو وہ اور اوسکے لڑکے اور اوسکي جورو اور جو اوسکے گھرانے سب بلا خرچ آنے پاوينگے - اور جو قلي ايک بار ٹاپو ہوکر ہندوستان ہوکر آيا ہوگا وہ پھر لوٹ آنيکا خرچ نہين پاويگا - جو قلي لگاتار رہکر پانچ برس پورا کريگا اور محنت کا کام کرنے کا سرٹيفيکٹ پاويگا يا پانے کا حقدار ہوگا وہ اپنے خرچ سے ہندوستان مين آنے سکيگا - جاتے وقت قلي کو گرم کپڑ اور کمبل مفت ملتا ہی آتے وقت مفت نہين -

جو کوئي قلي کوئي وقت ٹاپو چھوڑ کے چلا جاتا اگرچہ وہ ٹاپو مين دس برس پورا کيا ہوگا يا نہين وہ ہندوستان مين لوٹتے وقت ٹاپو کي طرف سے کوئي طرح کي مدد نہين پاويگا -

علاوہ شرطين — کالوني يا ٹاپو مين پہنچنے کے پيچھے ہر ايک پرديسي قلي کو اُنکے مالکون کے طرف سے پہلے تين مہينے تک کھانا جميکا گورنمنٹ کے ٹھہرائے ہوئے حساب سے ہر ہفتہ دو شلنگ چھہ پنس جو کہ آج کل ايک روپيہ چودہ آنے کے برابر ہی دينے سے ہر ايک کو جسکي عمر بارہ برس يا زيادہ ہی مليگا -

ہر ايک لڑکے يا لڑکي کو جسکي عمر ايک اور بارہ برس کے اندر ہی ہر ہفتہ ايک شلنگ تين پنس جو کہ آج کل پندرہ آنے کے برابر ہی دينے سے بڑونکا آدھا کھانا مليگا -

پرديسي قليون کو جو اقرار نامے کے بموجب ہين رہنے کے لايق گھر بلا کرايہ مليگا اور اُسکي مرمت مالک کے طرف سے بخوبي ہوا کريگي -

جب کوئي پرديسي قلي جو اقرار نامے کے بموجب ہی بيمار ہو جايگا تب اُسکو ہسپتال مين جگہہ مليگي اور - ڈاکٹر - دوا - بيمار کے لايق کھانا - معمولي کھانا - بلا قيمت مليگا -

I agree to accept the person named on the face of this form as an Emigrant on the above conditions.

In my presence.

W. B. Cumm[illegible]

Dated 28th August 1908.

Registering Officer at Cawnpore

Recruiter for JAMAICA.

C. BANKS, M. D.
Protector of Emigrants.

A. MARSDEN,
Government Emigration Agent for JAMAICA.

Contract of Indenture (Back)

India-An Early Civilization

Chapter 2

The earth has enough for every man's **NEED**, but not enough for every man's **GREED**.

The seven deadly sins are
wealth without work,
pleasure without conscience,
knowledge without character,
cause without morality,
science without humanity,
worship without sacrifice,
politics without principle.

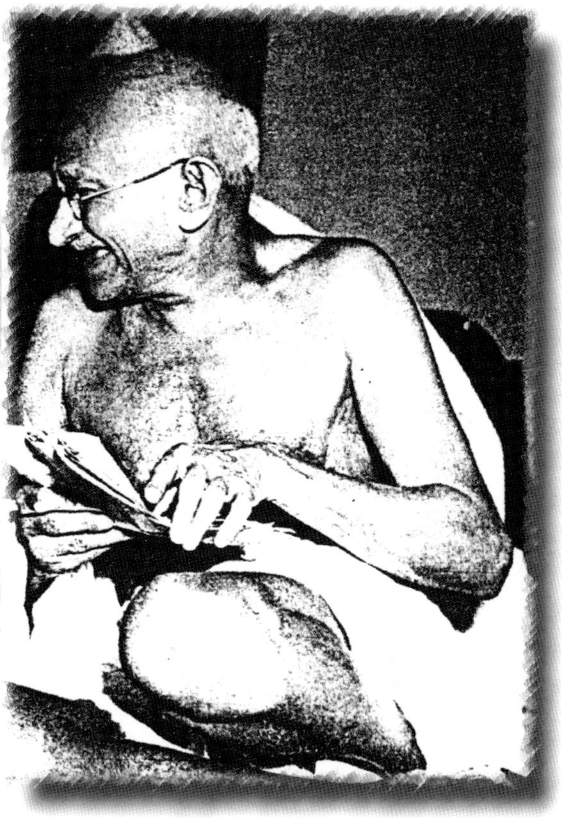

Mohandas K. Gandhi

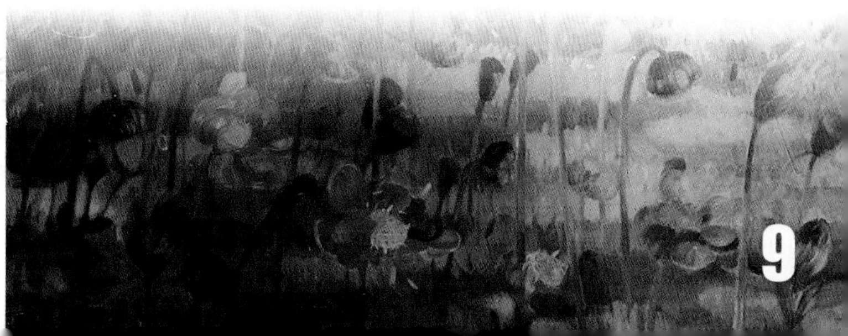

For hundreds of years, India meant mystery, wealth and excitement to the countries of the west. Early European explorers travelled to India for jewels, rugs, silks, spices and other valuable articles. Christopher Columbus was looking for a shorter and easier route to India when he arrived in the West Indies. Today India is no longer a wealthy nation. The rule of the British contributed greatly to India's poverty.

Throughout its history, India with its fine cities and prosperous villages, attracted the attention of foreign invaders. Indian history tells of wars and conquests, of achievement and the destruction of many beautiful Indian cities which were ravaged by war. The city of Lucknow is an example of a beautiful city destroyed by war. William Howard Russell was an Englishman who travelled through India in 1885--89. This is his description of Lucknow:

> "*More extensive than Paris and more brilliant . . . A vision of palaces, minars, domes azure and golden cupolas, colonnades, long facades of fair perspective in pillar and column, terraced roofs– all rising up amid a calm still ocean of the brightest verdure. Look for miles and miles away and still the ocean spreads . . . not Rome, not Athens, not Constantinople, not any city I have ever seen appears to me so striking and so beautiful as this.*"
>
> (Naipaul, *A Million Mutinies Now*, p 391)

Classical & Religious Works of India

The Hindu god Shiva as Nataraja, Lord of the Dance. Southern India, A.D. 1100's. Bronze. 1.54 m high.

Indian literature extends back over 3000 years, and includes great religious classics, oral poetry and modern verse and prose. Some of the classics include the Upanishads (spiritual teachings), the Mahabharata (the great wars of the Bharatas) and the Ramayana (story of Rama). The Mahabharata is the world's longest poem consisting of 100,000 verses. The Bhagavad Gita (The song of the Lord) is an excerpt from the Mahabharata, and describes the meaning of religious duty or

"dharma" for a Hindu person. The Ramayana, by the poet Valmiki, is another religious epic which tells stories depicting the battles between goodness and evil.

Since many Muslim dynasties ruled India there are many poems written in Persian. Indo-Persian poets wrote Gasidas or praise poems, and Ghazals or sequences of linked verse written in couplets. These were the stories and poems the East Indians brought with them to the Caribbean. One of the greatest names in modern Indian literature is Rabindranath Tagore who won the Nobel Prize for Literature in 1913. He translated into English his poetry collection, Gitanjali (song offerings).

Rabindranath Tagore

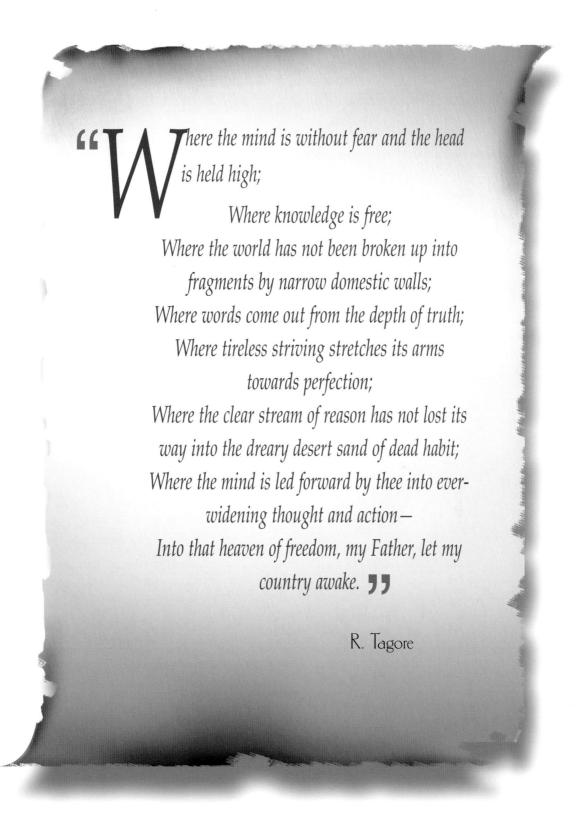

"Where the mind is without fear and the head
is held high;
Where knowledge is free;
Where the world has not been broken up into
fragments by narrow domestic walls;
Where words come out from the depth of truth;
Where tireless striving stretches its arms
towards perfection;
Where the clear stream of reason has not lost its
way into the dreary desert sand of dead habit;
Where the mind is led forward by thee into ever-
widening thought and action—
Into that heaven of freedom, my Father, let my
country awake."

R. Tagore

India in the late 1830s (Look Lai 1993: xiii)

Jawaharlal Nehru and Mohandas K. Gandhi, two leaders of the Independence movement in India. Nehru became India's first Prime Minister.

The British in India

The year 1715 is regarded as the starting point of the British Empire in India. However, large parts of the country still remained under the rule of the Indian princes. For the next hundred years the British extended their rule to more and more of India. The first prime minister of India, Jawaharlal Nehru, wrote that the position of the British in northern India was one of power and wealth without responsibility. *(Nehru 416)*

Nineteenth Century India

During the seventeenth and eighteenth centuries, Britain imported much more from India than it exported to that country. The main imports from India were cotton, silk, raw silk, tea, pepper, porcelain, gold and diamonds. The main exports to India were woollen and metal goods.

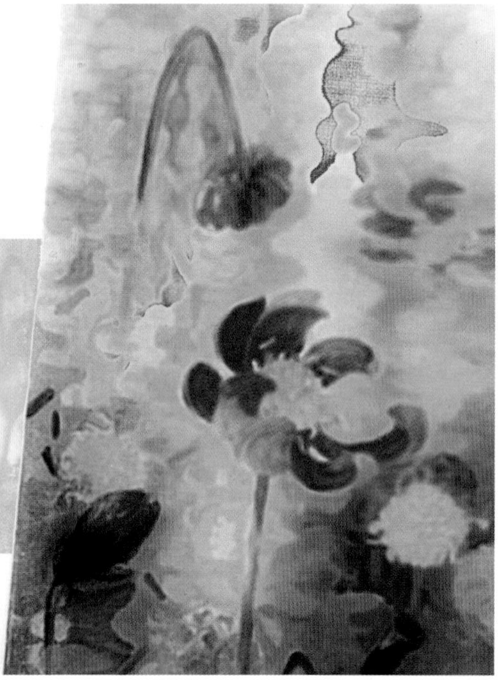

The textile industry is one of the oldest industries in India. The Indians developed the art of dyeing cloth using the "batik" method. Wax was poured over the fabric to form intricate patterns, and the fabric was then soaked in dye. With this method, the Indians produced fabrics with beautiful designs and colours. Other industries included carpet making, ceramics, ivory, wood carving and glass making, in addition to fine jewelry. These products of India attracted trade from the east and west. Merchants came to trade for cloth, jewelry, pottery, glassware and spices.

After the Industrial Revolution, Britain produced a greater quantity of manufactured goods and changed from being an importer of Indian goods to an exporter of manufactured goods to India.

After Britain established a strong political base in India in 1763, the traditional Indian village economy was organized to suit British imperialism. There were three major areas in the reorganisation:

(1) A new system of taxation which imposed greater hardships on the village economies.

(2) Introduction of a "landlord" class which brought great oppression to the Indian peasants.

(3) A trade policy which allowed free entry of British goods to India but put a heavy tax on Indian goods entering Britain.

This resulted in the abandonment of traditional Indian manufacturing and unemployment for millions of artisans. The Governor General of India, Lord William Bentinck, made this famous comment,

"The misery hardly finds a parallel in the history of commerce. The bones of the cotton weavers are bleaching the plains of India." (Look Lai 23)

In 1857, the Indian rulers united in one final effort to recover power and to drive out the British but this revolt failed and the British took direct charge. In the early days of the British in India, the merchants of the East India Company traded and plundered without any return to India. A great deal of wealth

went to help the industrial development of England at this vital period.

During the nineteenth century raw materials went from India to factories in England to produce English textiles. India was famous for its textile industry which produced fine cotton, silk and woollen goods. For many centuries Indian textiles were exported to Europe, China, Japan and parts of Africa. The British policy in India was to crush the Indian industry and bring in goods manufactured from England. The textile industry collapsed along with the shipbuilding and metalworking industries. This policy resulted in many artisans and craftsmen being out of work. They wandered through the towns and villages in search of employment. There were also periods of intense famine at this time which caused even greater distress in the overcrowded areas of India. These unemployed workers listened to the 'arkatis' or recruiters, who told them of new countries where work was available for good wages.

Famine in India.

For those 90 years of emigration, many of the emigrants exchanged one form of poverty in India for another in the West Indies. Some emigrants found only death and disease in the new land and never lived to return to India. The East Indians left their homes and families and provided cheap labour, so that the sugar planters could enjoy unparalleled prosperity.

Indian immigration finally ended due to protest by citizens of India and the West Indies.

TAJ MAHAL. The magnificent Taj Mahal has come to be synonymous with India. Marble, inlaid with precious stones in floral and calligraphic motifs, adorns the façade of the Taj Mahal.

At the turn of the 17th century, at the height of Mughal power, Agra was the imperial capital and the largest and most important city of Northern India. It was in this city that the Emperor Shahjahan built his monument to love. It is a memorial to his wife Muntaz Mahal, who died 18 months after he became Emperor.

Leaving INDIA

Chapter 3

Calcutta docks. This was the port from which most of the East Indians sailed for the West Indies

"In this modern era of rapid and easy travel, it is easy to forget the awful sufferings not only of enslaved Africans in the building of today's world but of those other millions as well who, driven by poverty or trapped by deceit, sacrificed their lives in building new worlds for their children."

Sidney Mintz
(Look Lai: xxviii)

During times of hardship in India people took advantage of the opportunity to emigrate, but when harvests were good they preferred to stay at home. They also had a fear of crossing the ocean (the kali-pani or black water) because this meant that an Indian would no longer be a member of his caste.

During the nineteenth century there were many famines in India and the failure of many industries because of the British policy. Many people wandered through the towns and villages looking for work. The recruiting agents went to the towns and villages and painted a picture of a good life in a new country where a worker could earn enough money in a few years and then return home. The recruiters looked for young men and women in good health, willing to travel to a distant land in search of a better life.

Sailing ships

Recruiting Indentured Labour for the Caribbean

Arrival in the West Indies. After their long journey, the East Indians wait to be sent to the different estates.

Most of the recruits for the Caribbean came from North India, from the districts of Basti, Fyzabad, Gonda and Gorakhpur in the United Provinces and Shahabad in Bihar. They sailed from the Port of Garden Reach in Calcutta. A smaller number came from Southern India and sailed from Madras.

The immigrants came from a number of castes. A caste is defined as a group of people having a specific social rank determined by occupation, descent or marriage. However, caste was more than just a social system, it was based on powerful religious beliefs and sanctions. Members of a caste have common occupations, and follow the same customs relating to marriage, food, and questions of pollution by members of lower castes. Caste members marry only members of their own caste, a practice known as endogamy. Only members of the same caste may eat together.

There are approximately 3,000 'jatis' or castes, and these are grouped loosely into four varnas. The four varnas are:

BRAHMINS:	*Priests, Scholars*
KSHATRIYAS:	*Warriors or Rulers*
VAISHYAS:	*Merchants, Traders, Farmers*
SUDRAS:	*Artisans, Labourers, Servants*
OUTVARNAS or UNTOUCHABLES:	*They were called "children of God" by Mohandas Gandhi.*

Since India gained independence, there have been many modifications of the caste system, and the Indian constitution has outlawed untouchability.

There was no attempt to recruit families. The planters needed steady and cheap labour and did not want to support children or the elderly. Most of the immigrants were young men or women.

Those who wanted to go to this new country were taken by a recruiting agent to a sub-depot where they were examined by a travelling doctor. If the recruit was declared satisfactory by the doctor, he/she then went to a registering officer for questioning and registration. The contract of indenture was signed in the presence of the registering officer and the name of the recruit and his or her caste, sex and village were listed on the contract.

The recruits were then taken to the immigration depot in Calcutta or Madras to wait for the ship on which they would travel. Many of the recruits never returned to India and never saw their family and friends again.

Waiting at the Depot

This journey from the Old World of the east to the New World was not easy. The old traditions were left behind and a new way of life was started. While they were waiting at the depot for the sailing date, all the recruits lived together as one community. The colonial authorities treated Hindus, Muslims, Brahmins and Sudras as equals. They did not make any distinctions for religion or caste. All the recruits ate together and shared common facilities for bathing and washing. The caste rules regarding food preparation and contamination started to break down from this point, and today Indians in the Caribbean do not follow the caste system.

The Journey

The long journey of 11,000 miles from India to the Caribbean crossed two oceans – the Indian Ocean and the Atlantic Ocean. During this time on the ship the recruits made friends with each other. They called each other 'jahajibhai' or 'jahajibahin', which meant shipbrother or shipsister. During their stay in the new country jahajis behaved like family towards each other.

This is a short account by the captain of a ship going from India to the Caribbean. He describes the food and clothing for his passengers:

> "*The coolies had their own cooks, in strict accordance with their caste or faith, though caste is in great measure broken down by the mere fact of their leaving India and coming to sea . . . They consumed a great amount of rice and curry . . . A much appreciated meal was a curry of rice and fresh mutton. The ship also supplied clothing – about three yards of calico for the men and about five yards for the women – but when getting in the vicinity of the Cape of Good Hope, a large woolen blanket was served to all of them as a extra precaution against the cold.*"
>
> (Angel 63)

Indentureship:
Life on the Estates Chapter 4

Group of East Indians in the Caribbean, late 19th century

"History is defined "not as records of monuments and empires in habitual celebration of domination and the humiliation of large hordes of humanity, but rather as a self-redeeming, self-accepting story of one's person, culture and of one's ultimate significance in the order of things."

(Caribbean Quarterly, 46: 3&4. 85)

On arrival in the new country each indentured immigrant was assigned to a particular estate. Indians had left India to work on the sugar, tea and rubber plantations of the British colonies, but work on the sugar estates was hardest. The price of sugar had fallen, and the profits were being cut. The estate owners paid the lowest wages possible so that they could ensure their profits.

Cutting cane. The sugar cane reaping season or "crop time" lasted from January to June. The labourers toiled in the burning sun for very low wages.

For 100 years the wages on the sugar estates in the Caribbean hardly moved. The Indians who migrated were a steady and cheap source of labour. The sugar industry kept the labourers hard at work by using a system of penalties and punishments.

PAY DAY ON THE ESTATE.
The Indian woman in the colony feels that she is independent of her husband as she has to earn her own living by working in the field and gets her weekly wages in her own hand (Dabydeen 232-3)

Work on the Estates

When the new immigrants lined up for work on the estates they were sorted into two groups. The stronger workers were given the job of digging, clearing and planting. The weaker workers

and the women would do the weeding around the young cane. The jobs were given out by 'task' and if a worker did not complete the task, he or she was not paid for that day. The wages for this kind of labour was one shilling per day, but few workers earned this.

The daily work started early, at 4:30 or 5:00 am during the crop season. In the middle of the morning half-an-hour was given for breakfast and then work resumed. Work was stopped at any time between 2:30 and 5:30 in the afternoon. This meant a working day of up to 10 or 12 hours in the burning sun.

The planters had many punishments for the labourers. In British Guiana, the local planters used to say that they would have their immigrants at work, in hospital or in jail. Special immigration laws regulated where an immigrant should live, where he/she should travel, the number of days and the hours he/she should work, and also the penalties to be paid for not obeying these laws.

Experience of Indentureship

In Cane Estate
Driver roughing people
Dey beating dem
Dey kicking dem
Dey doing all kinda ting
I cyan lie.

I cyan get one cent more
Twenty-five cents I wuking

Wha yu go do
You have to do; you have to make it out
If yu eh wuk
Dey go kick you
An dey do buff you every day
If you sick
If you sick go hospital
But if you nuh sick
You have to wuk bhai

We cyan whistle an
Sing in de wuk
Cyan whistle and sing E go say
Go in de blasted barrack
An sing
Not in my wuk

(Mahabir)

Translation

On the sugar estates
The supervisors abuse the workers
They beat them
and kick them
and many other things
I am not lying.

I cannot earn anymore
Than twenty-five cents although
I work and work
What could I do
You have to go on
If you don't work
they kick you
And they insult you every day
If you are sick
You could go to the hospital
But if you are not sick
You must work, my brother

We cannot whistle and
Sing while we work
We were told
Go in the blasted barracks
And sing
Not while you are working for me

This situation was very different from the life in the towns or villages of India where the immigrant lived before. On the estate they were just labourers employed in the sugar industry. They did not own the land or its produce. Their wages were their only reward, and this accounted for the "thriftiness" of the Indian labourer. They saved their money for the return to India and they were willing to forgo present comforts for future rewards.

Penalties and Restrictions

The immigrants lived a life similar to that of a prisoner in many ways. The worker could not leave the estate unless he had a 'pass', and if he was absent from work, he would be fined or sent to prison. In the industrial societies of Europe and America, a worker would not be paid if he was absent but on the sugar estates the Indians were convicted as criminals for this action.

In 1909 George Fitzpatrick, a Trinidad-born lawyer of East Indian parents, criticised the immigration regulations concerning the 'pass'. He said that it did not seem right that a man, who has done his daily work, should not have the right to visit a friend or relative, who may live on a neighboring plantation, without going through the ordeal of getting a written pass from his employer.

This is an excerpt from a story by Samuel Selvon about a "pass" from the estate.

"No thieves and vagabonds about for you to catch, but I think I see a coolie man down the road coming? My eyesight bad in the hot sun."

"Eh-heh?" Norbert put his hand to his forehead to shade the sunlight, and looked. "Like it was a coolie for true, and like he have a child with him. You right, Tanty! On the other side of the road!" Norbert liked public participation when he was called upon to do his duty: he pretended to be swayed by their reaction or opinion. So he raised his voice and shouted as Changoo and Raman drew near. "Aye, you coolie man! Come over here!" by the time the Indian and his son crossed the road, the gambling stopped, and the women vendors gathered around the gamblers and idlers. There was drama in the air. They liked to watch Norbert in action, and he liked to perform for them. Furthermore, they considered themselves more as participators than spectators in what was about to unfold.

"What you doing in town, coolie? You run away from the estate?"

Changoo was disconcerted by the crowd, and the black man in the police uniform.

Though he had his pass safely knotted in his dhoti, it was the first he had ever seen so many black people together.

"No, no," he said quickly.

"Where you from?"

"Cross crossing"

"Where your free paper? You got free paper?"

"Yes, yes." Changoo fumbled to undo the knot in his dhoti as the crowd laughed and jeered.

"He got it tie-up in he trousers!"

"You call that trousers? It look more like a sheet he got tie round he waist!" those in the background pressed forward to see what was happening.

Norbert took the pass Changoo handed him and held it at arm's length, drawing it closer and closer to his eyes. The crowd jostled and elbowed, eager for blood.

"Take him down, Norb, take him down!"

"Lock him and throw away the key!"

"H'mm," Norbert said, and "h'mm," and he frowned and rubbed his chin.

"Cross crossing, eh?"

Changoo was scared. The boy was gripping his arm tightly. He knew Raman was frightened, and that if he showed his own fear the boy's fright would turn to terror.

Nothing was wrong with his pass, but this policeman was acting as if he had run away.

Norbert now, slowly, took a notebook out of the breast pocket of his tunic. The crowd acted silent when the notebook appeared.

"I have to make a note of this." he licked the tip of the pencil.

"What your name is, Ram or Singh?"

"No Changoo."

"H'mm, that's a new one, how you spellit?"

Raman said, "C-h-a-n-g-o-o."

Norbert looked at the boy as if he seeing him for the first time.

"Oh, and what you call, boy?"

"I call Raman. R-a-m-a-n."

"Oho ! Well. Mr. Raman, this pass is only for Mr. Changoo. What you have to say about d-a-t?"

The witticism drew the laughter Norbert expected from his extras, and the inevitable comments.

"Is a spelling competition, Norb!"

"Ask him to spell policeman!"

"No, ask him to spell Bound-coolie!"

It seemed to Changoo that the mood was changing from antagonism to derision and suddenly his mood changed too, and he was angry. ”

(Birbalsingh 19-20)

Policemen had the power to stop any Indian immigrant and arrest him if he did not have his pass. In Trinidad, in one year alone 234 Indian immigrants were convicted for this offence and sent to prison. If the workers had problems with their employers, they had the right to appeal to the Protector of Immigrants. In order to make their appeal, they had to get a pass from a local magistrate who, in most cases, was a friend of the employer. In British Guiana, an indentured labourer, who went to Georgetown to give evidence against his employer, could be arrested and sent to jail for being absent from his estate.

INMATES IN TRINIDAD PRISONS
FOR BREACHES OF IMMIGRATION ORDINANCES

YEAR	NUMBER OF INMATES
1900	939
1901	1010
1902-3	1730
1903-4	1745
1904-5	2049
1905-6	1915
1906-7	1768
1907-8	1869

There were other laws passed to keep the Indian labourers under control. For the crime of arson, the labourer had to serve a sentence of 15 years and for burglary, he had to serve eight years hard labour.

In addition to the harsh conditions of work on plantations, there was also much illness due to poor living conditions. There was a high death rate on the estates, and many of the immigrants died after living one or two years in their new country. They never lived to complete their indentureship or return to India.

Some Caribbean planters abandoned those labourers who became ill. Since they had no family to take care of them, many of these abandoned labourers died, friendless, starving and alone.

In the West Indies, there were few large scale riots, lengthy strikes, or violent opposition from indentured labourers. However, there were some incidents by the labourers expressing protest against excessive work, unpaid wages, or unfair treatment. In most cases, the official from the estate was believed, and the indentured labourers were punished.

In 1914, at Worthy Park, St. Catherine, Jamaica, the Inspector of Immigration arrested the ringleader of a strike. The other workers attacked the officials with sticks and hoes, and many of those involved in the strike were sent to prison.

In 1869, in British Guiana, there were riots and violence on the following plantations -- La Jalousie, Lenora Malgre Tout, Mahaicony and Enterprise. Walton Look Lai writes

> *"the use of armed force to quell worker discontent occurred on several occasions in British Guiana, the most well known incidents being at Devonshire Castle in 1872, NonPareil in 1896, Friends in 1902, Lusignan in 1912 and Rose Hall in 1913. All of them resulted in loss of life among the Indians. The Rose Hall clashes ending with 15 dead. The strike at Friends arose directly out of grievances over sexual exploitation of the Indian women by managers and overseers."*
>
> (Look Lai 145)

During the final years of indenture, the Indians, especially the return migrants, became more militant. In Trinidad, there were strikes at Harmony Hall, Orange Grove, Nonpareil, Waterloo, Camden and Caroni. In 1907, two overseers were beaten to death at Waterloo and Perseverance estates, one at each estate.

These acts of resistance showed that the Indians were not all docile and passive, and tried to fight against the injustices meted to them.

Among the indentured immigrants, there were few who were educated or equipped to challenge the colonial authorities. 'Bechu' was an extraordinary indentured labourer. He is described as follows:

> *"Only one East Indian in the whole nineteenth century appeared as a potential leader [in British Guiana]. He was unique in that he was not of the local East Indian middle class, and he championed the cause of the down trodden sugar worker. His name was Bechu, a Bengali who came to the colony as an indentured immigrant. He became the first East Indian to address a Royal Commission [in February 1897]. Not surprisingly, he did not obtain his early education in British Guiana. He was educated in India by a missionary. His public criticisms in the newspapers of the sugar planters and his defence of the labourers brought him into conflict with the plantation authorities."*
>
> (Ramnarine 233)

Religious and Social Life

Chapter 5

"We were immemorially people of the countryside, far from the courts of princes, living according to rituals we didn't always understand and yet were unwilling to dishonour because that would cut us off from the past, the sacred earth, the gods."

(Naipaul, Enigma of Arrival 351)

The indentured labourers came from many different castes. Brahmins, Rajput and Chattri – the higher castes – came in small numbers. Many immigrants came from the following castes – Ahirs (cow minders) Kurmi (cultivators) Kumhar (potters) and Chamar (leather workers) – and they were used to agricultural labour. On each shipload, a minority of Muslims arrived.

Most of the Indians were either agricultural labourers or small farmers. In the West Indies, they formed a closed rural community with their own religion and social customs. Many of the immigrants spoke the Bhojpuri dialect of North India and this soon became a common language for all the Indians throughout the West Indies.

Worshippers on the plantation

Many villagers knew verses from the Hindu scriptures or the Holy Koran. After work, in the evenings, they met in small groups and chanted verses of scriptures. The Hindu immigrants

Muslim worshippers leaving the mosque in a village in Trinidad, 2000.

also worshiped their deities in their homes or in their temples and the Muslims prayed in their mosques. This is a description, by a Christian missionary, of worship by Muslims:

"A company of twelve or fifteen men, who have met together for prayer. They stood in a line, all dressed alike in tight-fitting white garments, and nicely adjusted turbans. At a given signal all hands were raised, and the first prayer was offered with the palms upward and the thumbs of each hand touching the tip of the corresponding ear. The second was offered with hands across the breast and with bowed heads; a third prayer was spoken with hands on their knees; a fourth by all on their knees, and the fifth and last was offered on their knees and with their foreheads touching the ground. The scene was most impressive, and could be witnessed every Friday, whenever there was a Mohammedan group."

(Ramesar 104)

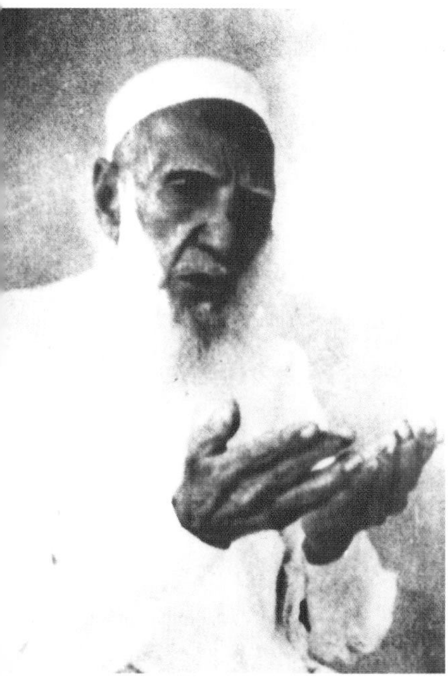

Haji Ruknadeen: a Muslim religious leader in the nineteen twenties

The Muslims also celebrated the festival of Eid-ul-Fitr to mark the end of fasting during the holy month of Ramadan. The Shiite Muslims celebrated the occasion of Muharran also called Tadjah or Hosay. This was the most popular religious observance celebrated during indentureship by both Muslims and Hindus. The annual Muharran celebration marked the death of Hassan and Hosein, the grandsons of the prophet Mohammed. The Tazias (tadjahs) were models of the tombs of these brothers. The observance of Muharran lasted ten days, and ended with a grand street procession. All the tadjahs were carried along the street in a slow procession, accompanied by the beating of tassa drums. Women chanted and wailed, and the men engaged in mock stick fights, shouting "Hassan" and "Hosein." This celebration offered to the labourers some release from the hard work and confinement of the plantations.

The Muharram Massacre

On the 30th October 1884, there occurred in Trinidad one of the most traumatic incidents during the history of indentureship. It took place during the observance of Muharran. The British colonial police, with the support from British soldiers, opened fire on the Muharran processions. Sixteen persons were killed, and over 100 injured. There was some unrest on the plantations at this time and the colonial government wanted to provoke a confrontation with the Indians and to give them a bloody lesson in obedience to the law.

The Indians prepared for Muharran and put the final touches on their tadjas. They heard rumours of police preparation, but few believed the police would really shoot them. In south Trinidad the processions from the estates of Wellington, Picton, Lennon, Rowbottom, Retrench and Union joined together and proceeded into San Fernando. At the entrance to Cipero Street, the magistrate, Mr. Child, read the Riot Act in English to the Indians, most of whom could not understand English. He then gave the order to the police to fire straight into the crowd.

At the Mon Repos Junction in San Fernando, a similar shooting occurred. The New Era newspaper reported that:

> *"the news of the slaughter of coolies, has caused a sensation in Port-of Spain, where public opinion does not approve of the policy. The government are deemed to have acted with haste and undue severity."*
>
> (Singh 22-23)

Omaid, a Hindu on Petit Morne estate stated, during the court inquiry:

> "*I come from Oude, about a day's journey, from Lucknow, and have been here for more than three years. On the 30th October I was in the procession and had heard there were orders forbidding the processions to go on the road, to leave the estate or to go to San Fernando. We did not leave the estate. Petit Morne extends right up to San Fernando, and we were shot before we left the estate; two gentlemen came and told us to stop. They had a book with them. We said we will not cross the boundary when we saw the police drawn up, we stopped and asked for four men to carry the tadja, whilst the others remained behind, they replied, "no, the tadjas will not be allowed to go through San Fernando." After this answer, the procession did not go any further it only stopped where it was. Boodhoosingh who had come to remonstrate with the coolies was told that to get out of the way as the police were going to fire. I was standing by the side of the tadja, and when the police fired, the wounded men fell, and the others ran away. Although I am a Hindu, I accompanied the procession, as is the custom for all coolies in Trinidad to do so. We did not mean to go through San Fernando. We were quite content to follow orders if they would only give us some place to throw the tadjas.*"
>
> (Singh 128)

Some of the festivals which were celebrated in the villages of India were not celebrated in the West Indies during indentureship. Divali, the festival of lights, only became popular after the abolition of indentureship. Holi or Phagwa, celebrating the beginning of spring was always popular. The immigrants sang and danced to the music of the tassa drums, and splashed each other with abir, a red liquid.

Hindu temple built by East Indians in the nineteenth century, in Port Mourant, Guyana.

The planters gave only a few holidays for religious festivals and a few provided building materials for Hindu temples and mosques. In Guyana, there were two temples and no mosques in 1870, but there were 52 temples and 50 mosques by 1920.

In the villages, traditional marriage ceremonies were celebrated according to the Hindu and Muslim rites. These were large marriage processions from village to village with music, song and dancing. The wedding party and guests wore a lot of gold and silver jewellery and great feasts were held.

This is a description of a bride and groom in 1893:

> *"The grooms were two coolies in full Indian costumes. On their heads were kinds of turbans a little like the Basque beret, and decorated with ribbons, gold paper, etc. on the ears- several gold pendants. Their gold fringed robe was floor length, with a magnificent belt holding it around the hips. The costume of the two brides was no less picturesque. Their corsage of scarlet velvet contrasted tastefully with the whiteness of their dresses. Their bare arms were covered with silver ornaments, and their fingers covered with different kinds of rings. Around the neck they wore a large collar made from some twenty silver pieces. Besides earings, they wore the most magnificent ornaments that I could see, in spite of the veils hiding their faces. These were gold necklaces with jewels of gold or precious stones. This necklace hung down to the chin and completely encircled the mouth."*
>
> (Ramesar 113)

However, these marriages celebrated by Hindu priests or Muslim imams were not considered legal. As a result, the children from these marriages were not considered legitimate and could not inherit property from their parents.

Other methods of relaxation for the indentured labourers were the drinking of rum and the smoking of ganja. There were many rum shops near the estates and the village rum shop was an important social centre. There was much debate about the smoking of ganja or bhang, but the final decision was to let the Indians smoke the ganja, but at a very high price.

Hindu priests, 1890s

INDIAN Women

Chapter 6

"We hold these truths to be self evident; that all men **and women** are created equal."

(Elizabeth Cady Stanton)

In 1845, the ship *"Fath al Rozack,"* landed in Trinidad with 206 men and 21 women as labourers. During the period Indian indentureship there was always a shortage of women. There was no encouragement for families to migrate or for women to migrate. Women were supposed to be naturally weak and not a good source of labour.

In nineteenth century India, a female child spent her youth preparing for marriage. She was trained in household duties only, and was taught that she must obey her husband. Her parents arranged marriage to a man of the same caste and she was sent to her husband's family home.

In 1915, the commissioners McNeil and Lal described the type of women who came to the Caribbean.

> *"The women who came out consist of one-third married women, who accompany their husbands, the remainder being mostly widows or women who have run away from their husbands or have been put away by them . . . the great majority are not, as they are frequently represented to be, shamelessly immoral. They are women who have gotten into trouble and apparently emigrate to escape from a life of promiscuous prostitution . . ."*
>
> (Cotton 372)

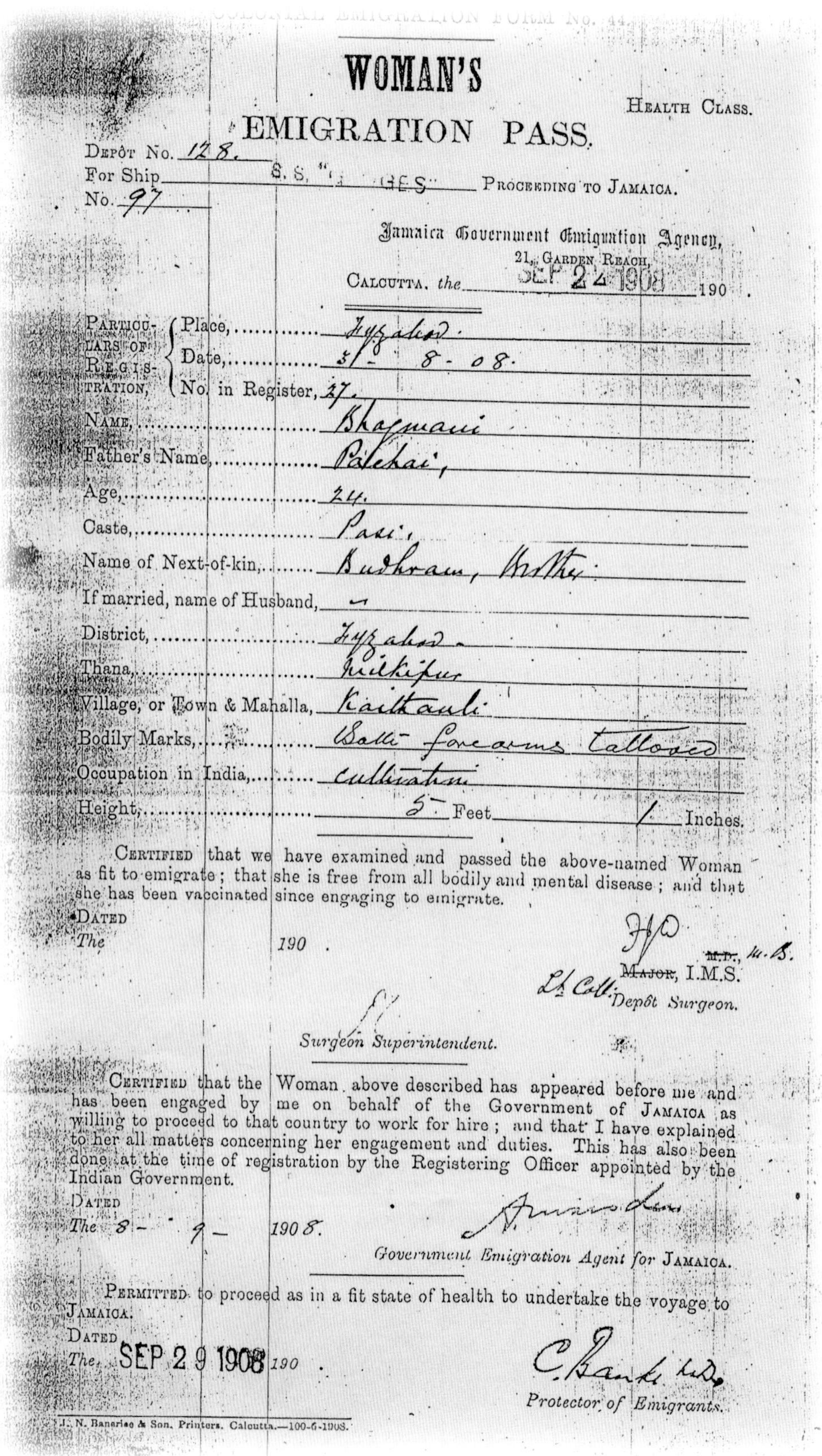

COLONIAL EMIGRATION FORM No. 44.

WOMAN'S EMIGRATION PASS.

HEALTH CLASS.

DEPÔT No. 128.
For Ship S. S. "[illegible]GES" PROCEEDING TO JAMAICA.
No. 97

Jamaica Government Emigration Agency,
21, GARDEN REACH,
CALCUTTA, the SEP 24 1908 190

PARTICULARS OF REGISTRATION, Place,	Fyzabad.
Date,	31 - 8 - 08.
No. in Register,	27.
NAME,	Bhagmani
Father's Name,	Palchai,
Age,	24.
Caste,	Pasi,
Name of Next-of-kin,	Budhram, brother
If married, name of Husband,	–
District,	Fyzabad.
Thana,	Milkipur
Village, or Town & Mahalla,	Kaithauli
Bodily Marks,	Both forearms tattooed
Occupation in India,	cultivation
Height,	5 Feet 1 Inches.

CERTIFIED that we have examined and passed the above-named Woman as fit to emigrate; that she is free from all bodily and mental disease; and that she has been vaccinated since engaging to emigrate.

DATED
The 190 .

Lt. Col. ~~MAJOR~~, ~~M.D.~~, M.B. I.M.S.
Depôt Surgeon.

Surgeon Superintendent.

CERTIFIED that the Woman above described has appeared before me and has been engaged by me on behalf of the Government of JAMAICA as willing to proceed to that country to work for hire; and that I have explained to her all matters concerning her engagement and duties. This has also been done at the time of registration by the Registering Officer appointed by the Indian Government.

DATED
The 8 - 9 - 1908.

Government Emigration Agent for JAMAICA.

PERMITTED to proceed as in a fit state of health to undertake the voyage to JAMAICA.

DATED
The SEP 29 1908 190 .

C. Banks
Protector of Emigrants.

J. N. Banerjee & Son, Printers, Calcutta.—100-6-1908.

Emigration pass for a young woman. She left India and went to the West Indies, alone.

It is likely that these single women emigrated because they suffered ill treatment in their homes. Perhaps they ran away from home and finally found themselves in a town where they were recruited as indentured labourers. In the case of widows, they were forbidden to remarry and were forced to live a life of misery with their in-laws.

East Indian women. The Indians did not have much confidence in banks. Their wages of silver and gold coins were melted and made into beautiful jewelry, worn by the women.

The planters created a gender division of labour, and women were given "light" tasks which were the most menial and the lowest paid. However, a missionary in British Guiana noted that in the colony the indentured woman felt that she was independent of her husband as she had to earn her living working in the field and got her weekly wages in her own hand. In a few cases, the best women workers earned as much as the average man. Even after the period of indentureship women continued working on the estates, and did not sit idly at home. Because they were financially independent, women were reluctant to put up with ill treatment. Single women were free to choose their husbands. An Indian woman in Trinidad told the missionary Sarah Morton

> *"When the last ship came I took a Papa. I will keep him as long as he treats me well. If he does not treat me well, I shall send him off at once."*
>
> (Dabydeen 233)

The most important fact affecting the Indian woman was her scarcity. The immigration laws recommend a ratio of two women to five men during indentureship, but the actual number of women immigrants was always less. The system of marriage underwent a major change because of this shortage. Instead of the dowry, which the bride's family gave to the bridegroom, the bridegroom gave the dowry to the bride. This shortage also caused lamentable quarrels and wife murders among Indians despite various preventative measures. In British Guiana, the statistics show 34 wife murders between 1859 and 1870 and 36 between 1884 and 1895. In Trinidad,

East Indian woman working on the sugar cane estate, late twentieth century

East Indian woman preparing food. She is using a "chulha", which is a U-shaped fireplace, made of clay and cow dung. Firewood was used for fuel.

between 1859 and 1863, there were 27 wife murders. However, as the ratio of the sexes improved, the rate of wife murders fell.

After indentureship many Indians moved away from the estates and settled in villages, where many aspects of traditional Indian culture were restored. Adaptations of the caste system, the joint family, and male and female roles were practised once more. The Indian custom of child marriage was restored and this meant that girls were withdrawn from school as soon as the marriage was arranged. Some women worked on family land instead of the estates, but in this case her labour was unrecognised and unpaid.

In the Caribbean, Indian women were the last to benefit from the education system. The Presbyterian missionaries and the Quakers had established many schools for the education of the Indians in Trinidad and British Guiana. However many Indian girls were denied education because of family practices and beliefs. In Trinidad, the statistics show that in 1903 there were 70 boys to every 30 girls in the Canadian Mission school. Twenty years later in 1923, the pattern was largely unchanged. It was not until the late 1930s that girls started attending school regularly. A very few women became teachers or owned property.

East Indian girl. They melt their silver coins and wear them on their arms and ankles, also string them around their necks till they look quite weighted down. Ear –rings, nose-rings, head bands, etc are often made with gold, and with very delicate workmanship, by their own countrymen.

In the middle of the twentieth century, Hindu and Moslem schools were established by religious organisations, and all Indian girls were given an opportunity for education. For more than 100 years, many Indian women were excluded from education. However, this situation has now changed and many Indian girls are receiving education at both the secondary and tertiary levels.

TRINIDAD

Chapter 7

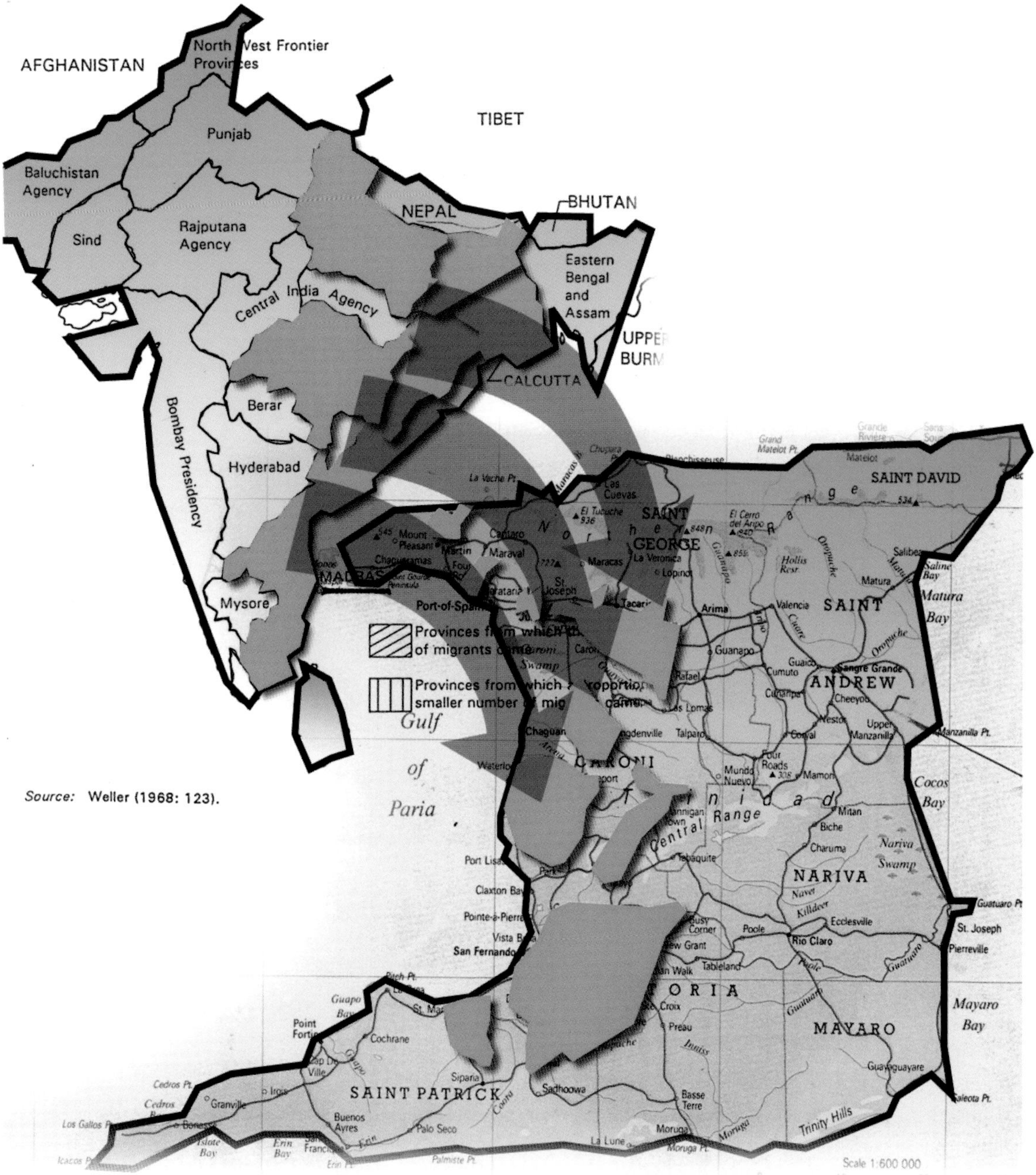

Source: Weller (1968: 123).

Ignorance of our history, we fear, is the cause of all misunderstandings and discords. I breaking with past, ignorance deprives us of the lessons of wisdom, drawn from earlier misfortunes. It is ignorance which makes us indisposed to one another. Therefore, let us know who we are, and in the spirit of understanding know that unity does not result from placing side by side perfectly identical bodies, but more from the fusion of diverse matters having affinity between themselves. (Pierre-Gustave Louis Bore, 1876)

(In Celebration, Frontispiece)

East Indian bride, wearing traditional Indian bridal garments.

Social Classes in Nineteenth Century Trinidad

In the nineteenth century, Trinidad, like other Caribbean islands, had three main social groups. At the top were the British and French estate owners who were the most powerful. In the middle were the 'free coloureds' and the 'free black' and the third class was made up of the ex-slaves and their descendants. At the end of slavery, many new ethnic groups emigrated to Trinidad.

People from the Eastern Caribbean came to Trinidad as well as African indentured labourers. Many Venezuelan labourers and peasants, the 'cocoa panyols', settled on the island, as did Portuguese from Madeira. Portuguese and Lebanese also left their homeland and emigrated to Trinidad. From Asia came the largest group, comprising 143,000 Indians, and 2,000 Chinese.

Each group made a distinct contribution to society and Trinidad today is a multi-ethnic society, with a rich and varied culture.

When the Indians arrived as immigrants to Trinidad they formed a new social group, a fourth group in the social structure. They were not welcomed by the other groups in the society and were not willing to mix with the other groups because of their beliefs of caste, religion and society. After their period of indentureship was over, most of the Indians decided to remain in Trinidad.

After 1870 Indians were entitled to free grants of land in exchange for their return passage. Twenty-seven village settlements arose because of this programme. These villages did not prosper because the lands that were granted to the Indians were not fit for cultivation. However, the Indians used their savings to purchase crown lands, and they established themselves as independent cultivators near the estates, or in small villages. They tried to establish an Indian way of life. They wanted to be as independent as possible and so they saved their money to buy small plots of crown lands or to rent lands for their own cultivation. By 1916, when the system of indenture was about to be stopped, the colonial government suspended the sale of crown lands to Indians. They also raised the price of swamp lands which the Indians were using to cultivate rice. By 1938, the price of swamp lands was three times the price of good land because the Government wanted to stop the growth of the rice industry so that the Indians would be dependent on the sugar estates.

This is a description of a village by the Christian missionary, John Morton.

"Our Village

It consisted of two rows of cottage homes, one on each side of the main road, our own premises and those of the Ward school occupying their place in the line and contributing an air of respectability to the whole. Most of the homes were little mud-plastered huts with thatched roofs of grass or cane leaves. A few of better class were built of wood and covered with galvanized iron. In some of these lived the elders and members of our congregation. On one side, that fronting the mission house, the canes of Malgretout Estate narrowed the view and approached very nearly the line of the cots. Behind us the land was more broken, affording a somewhat wider view of the fields of Corial Estate. There were a few small shops with a rather more pretentious one kept by a Chinaman, offering rum and groceries for sale. Squalor and dirt there were, but so veiled by kind nature with luxuriance of vegetation as to render the whole a not unpleasant scene.

In the mornings there was little stir in the village. Later many homely scenes were enacted at the doorsteps. Women might be seen washing the family clothing, husking rice by pounding it in a mortar, perhaps grinding corn in true Scriptural fashion turning one flat stone upon another, often singing as they turned. A mother grabs a naked child and pours over it a bucket of water, using her hand by way of a sponge. A man is being shaved or having his hair cut; another is engaged in goldsmith work, with his customers squatting around carefully watching lest he mix any baser metal with their coins which he is turning into jewelry for them. Such were the homes of the people the missionary had come to serve."

(Morton. 49)

Early Villages in Trinidad

The majority of the Indians remained in and around the sugar belt and battled for survival. They cut back on their expenses, tried to accumulate enough money to buy land and to build a home, and some tried to give their children a head start with

education. Many Indian homes had a vegetable garden, chickens and ducks or a few cows and goats. Up till 1950, the growing of their own rice provided an important food item. Many homes had rice stored for future use and in times of need this rice could be sold to help family finances.

The first homes constructed by the Indians were simple structures with mud-plastered walls and floor and a thatched roof. A special kind of clay mixed with cow dung was used to plaster or 'lepay' the floor.

As the family acquired more money, more extensive building materials were used, and today many Indian homes are spacious brick and concrete dwellings with beautiful lawns and gardens. After indentureship some Indians tried to escape the harsh life on the plantations and some of them ventured to Port-of-Spain and smaller towns. They opened small stores and shops or became market vendors. A few went into transport, first buying horse-drawn buggies, and then, later on, trucks and motor cars. However most of the Indians remained as rural agricultural labourers or peasants. Their earnings were less than the other groups in the society and their standard of living was lower. Up till 1950, many villages had no electricity, or regular pipe-borne water. However, many villages prospered during the 'oil boom' of the nineteen seventies and most homes now have running water, electricity and modern appliances.

Education

In order to improve their lot in life, many Indians turned to education. They had neglected education before because many of them were born in India, and came as adults to Trinidad. Their main concern was their labour and saving money to return to India to spend their last days. They could not spend the time and were not motivated to educate themselves or their children in an English education system. Throughout the first half of the twentieth century, Indians remained a rural population in Trinidad, with most of them in the sugar growing areas in Caroni and Victoria counties. In 1868 Rev John Morton, a Canadian missionary, visited Trinidad and found that there were approximately 20,000 East Indians from Madras and

SUSAMACHAR CHURCH. "The new building was opened on July 7 1872, and named "Susamachar" or Gospel" church. The church is constructed of the best building materials offered in the market here. Public opinion recognizes it as an ornament to the town...The very large assembly of people from every grade in society, representing many nations, and speaking many languages, was a public declaration of the very deep interest taken in the dedication of the first Christian place of worship erected for the 24,000 Asiatics in this colony. Mr. Morton opened the service in the Hindustani language, with praise, reading of the Scriptures and prayer. (Morton 104)

Calcutta. He thought they needed spiritual guidance, especially about Christianity. Rev Morton decided that he would start a mission to convert and educate Indians and the legacy today is the Presbyterian primary schools found in many Trinidad villages. The Presbyterian missionaries gained the confidence of the Indians by learning their language and customs. Rev John Morton had a printing press in Tunapuna where he printed religious material. Church services were conducted in Hindi, and early churches were given Hindi names, for example, Susamachar Presbyterian Church (San Fernando), Aramalaya Presbyterian Church (Tunapana).

In 1868, the Canadian missionaries started to establish schools for Indian children. These schools were first called Canadian Mission (C.M.) Schools and were later referred to as Presbyterian schools. By 1913, 40 out of 43 special schools were Presbyterian and 90% of the Indians were enrolled in these schools. In 1892, a Presbyterian theological college was opened for the training of local catechists and teachers and in 1894 the Naparima Teachers Training College was established. In 1899, a group of Indians who were mainly Christians, with some Hindus and Muslims, petitioned the Rev K.J. Grant for the opening of a secondary school and Naparima College was started. Christians as well as the sons of prosperous Muslims and Hindus attended and they became a new class of clerical and professional Indians. In 1945, 139 of 233 Indians described as had attended Presbyterian schools.

CANADIAN MISSION SCHOOLS—RETURN OF ATTENDANCE FOR 1909.

San Fernando District.

Schools.	On Roll.			
	Boys.	Girls.	Total.	Average Daily.
Bien Venue	73	31	104	54
Bonne Aventure	108	32	140	80
Canaan	107	26	133	72
Corinth	90	55	145	85
Dewi	68	20	88	54
Fyzabad	145	31	176	94
Harmony Hall	75	28	103	58
Hermitage	58	31	89	52
Rusillac	74	21	95	44
San Fernando	171	85	256	146
St. Madeleine	58	41	99	60
Siparia	95	13	108	57
Vistabella	79	64	143	81
Penal	97	39	136	70
Rock River	61	34	95	47
San Francique	30	21	51	21
Monkey Town	30	11	41	28
Total	1,419	583	2,002	1,103

However, even with the establishment of these schools attendance was poor, and the attendance of Indians was the lowest in the island. The enrollment was 70% male to 30% female and for many years Indian women were not given a chance for education. In 1921, only 12.6% of the total Indian population could read and write.

Graduate- Naparima Girls High School

In 1912 the Canadian missionaries took a bold step and founded the Naparima Girls High School. Rev Idris Hamid of the Presbyterian Church described it as

> *"a daring and progressive move. It was indicative of a determination to create a new people, with new values, lifestyles, faith and equipment, for there was nothing comparable to this in the tradition of the Indians."* (Ramesar, 110)

Many Indian women today are graduates of Neparima Girls High School and are to be found in many fields of employment. In later years, more secondary schools, St. Augustine Girls High school and the Hillview College were established by the Presbyterian school board. Today Indians place great value on education and are on the same education level as other groups in the population.

However many Indians were reluctant to give up their ancestral beliefs and accept Christianity. There were regular visits by Hindu and Muslim missionaries from India to Trinidad, and a new awareness and pride in the religions and languages of India.

Vedic elementary school, built by a Hindu organization in Trinidad.

Initially, a few schools were opened which taught Indian languages and religions, but these schools had very basic accommodation. Government aid was needed, and the Indians needed to form legal, religious organisations. There was disunity among both Hindus and Muslims, and it was only in 1949, that the first Indian non-Christian school was established -- the El Socorro Islamic School. During the 1950s, 12 primary schools were built by Muslim organisations, and approximately 48 by Hindu organisations.

The organisations also established secondary schools. The ASJA Girls High School, ASJA College and the Lakshmi Girls High School are the three secondary schools established by the Hindu and Muslim organisations.

The establishment of the schools helped in the education of East Indian women because most parents realised that education was now an asset for their daughters.

JAMAICA

Chapter 8

It would be disgraceful to any country to allow its inhabitants, under any circumstances short of general plague and famine, to be reduced to such a state of wretchedness as these poor people are in, but it is barbarous in a Christian country to drag human beings from their native land of plenty, and then to suffer them to sink in to so abject a state of starvation and wretchedness, as these coolies are reduced to.

(Falmouth Post, 20 July 1847)

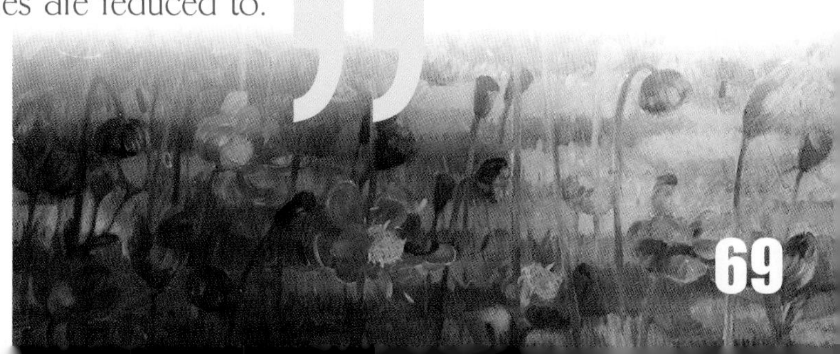

Between 1845 and 1916 approximately 37,000 East Indians came to Jamaica as indentured labourers. They were sent to estates mainly in the parishes of St. Andrew, St Mary, Portland, Clarendon, Westmoreland St Catherine and St Thomas. In Trinidad and Guyana, large numbers of Indians were sent to each estate. In Jamaica, a much smaller number was distributed to many estates. Some estates received only four indentured labourers while others received as many as 63.

Commemorative Stamps .

The first East Indian immigrants arrived in Jamaica on 9th May 1845 aboard the *"Blundell Hunter."* They disembarked at Old Harbour and were sent from there to the different estates.

These immigrants proved satisfactory and in 1846--47 approximately 4,000 more East Indians arrived. However, the Sugar Duties Act was passed and the preferential tariff for West Indian Sugar was abolished. This caused a depression in the sugar industry in the Caribbean. In Jamaica, the number of sugar estates in operation fell from 513 in 1846 to 427 in 1852. This caused a lot of suffering for the East Indian labourers. The only way they could survive was to go from estate to estate begging for employment. Some went to the towns, were unable to find work, and they turned to begging. Indian beggars were part of the scene in these towns.

In 1851, the indentureship system was started again because of the exodus of Jamaican labourers to work on the Panama canal. Some Indians in Jamaica also re-emigrated to other countries where they saw a chance for a better life. Between 1832 and 1930, over 4,000 Indians left Jamaica for Cuba, Mexico, Panama, Trinidad and Guyana.

During the first period of settlement, Indians in Jamaica suffered low wages and loss of employment when the sugar and banana industries were depressed. After 1930, this situation became worse due to the worldwide economic depression. The sugar and banana industries were particular affected. Abandonment of the sugar estates in the nineteen thirties and forties left many Indian estate workers without jobs.

Wash Day by the river

Post Indentureship

After the period of indentureship, some of the Indians moved away from the estates and came into the towns. They continued in agricultural occupations and their main source of income was market gardening. They grew a variety of vegetables, including cabbage, callaloo, eggplant and lettuce, and also plantains and flowers. These were sold in turn to the Chinese shops, or sold by women who carried the produce in baskets balanced on their heads. Some Indian men worked as casual labourers, and some Indian women worked as domestic helpers. A few Indians became jewellers, barbers, tailors and shopkeepers.

Education

Until 1899 no special schools were established for the East Indians who were reluctant to send their children to the local schools. The majority of the schools were Christian and religious education was a major part of the curriculum. Both Hindus and Muslims were opposed to this religious education in schools. Also, some of the Indians on the estates could not speak English and could not benefit from attending local schools.

The Quakers opened a special school at Orange Bay in 1899 and about 30--40 East Indian children attended. The Quakers also established schools at Fellowship in Portland, and Orange Hill estate in St Mary. Female teachers, who were paid by the government, taught both Hindi and English.

From 1891--1949 planters supported the attempt to educate Indian children. The colonial authorities realised that once the East Indians learnt English, they adjusted more easily to their environment. They could therefore be more easily integrated into the larger society. The proprietor for the estate "Ewings Caymanas" supported the school operated by the Presbyterians. He maintained the school and paid the minister. Industrial schools, homes and orphanages were also established for Indian children. "Restview" in Westmoreland, "Lyndale Girls Home" and "Swift Home" in St. Mary were some of the special institutions for Indian children. "Wortley Home" or the Constant Spring East Indian Orphanage was opened by Rev Canon Wortley exclusively for East Indians.

"The WORTLEY HOME" Kingston, Jamaica was built to care for East Indian orphans.

In 1929, the *SS Sutej* took the last shipload of Indians back to India. Thereafter, all the East Indians and their descendants settled in Jamaica. They were now regarded as permanent citizens of Jamaica and special educational institutions were not continued for them. After 1930 the special Indian schools were closed due to lack of funds, or they admitted non-Indian children. The East Indians in Jamaica now began to enter the government school system. However, up to 1945 the Indians in Jamaica had the highest illiteracy rate and the Indian organisations encouraged parents to send their children to school.

Since there was a smaller Indian population in Jamaica, more cultural practices were discontinued. Indians were a small minority in all settlements and were often in contact with the Afro-Jamaican majority. They adopted the language, the dress and many food habits of this majority. Because of the shortage of women, there was also a higher incidence of mixed marriages in Jamaica. In 1948, out of 56 marriages performed, one in five were mixed. The children of these marriages preferred things "Jamaican" to things "Indian".

East Indians are a small community in Jamaica today. They have retained some of the social and religious customs which their ancestors brought from India.

Banyan tree, Kingston, Jamaica. These trees were brought from India to the Caribbean. They grow more in circumference than height, and may reach up to 1500 feet in circumference.

GUYANA

Chapter 9

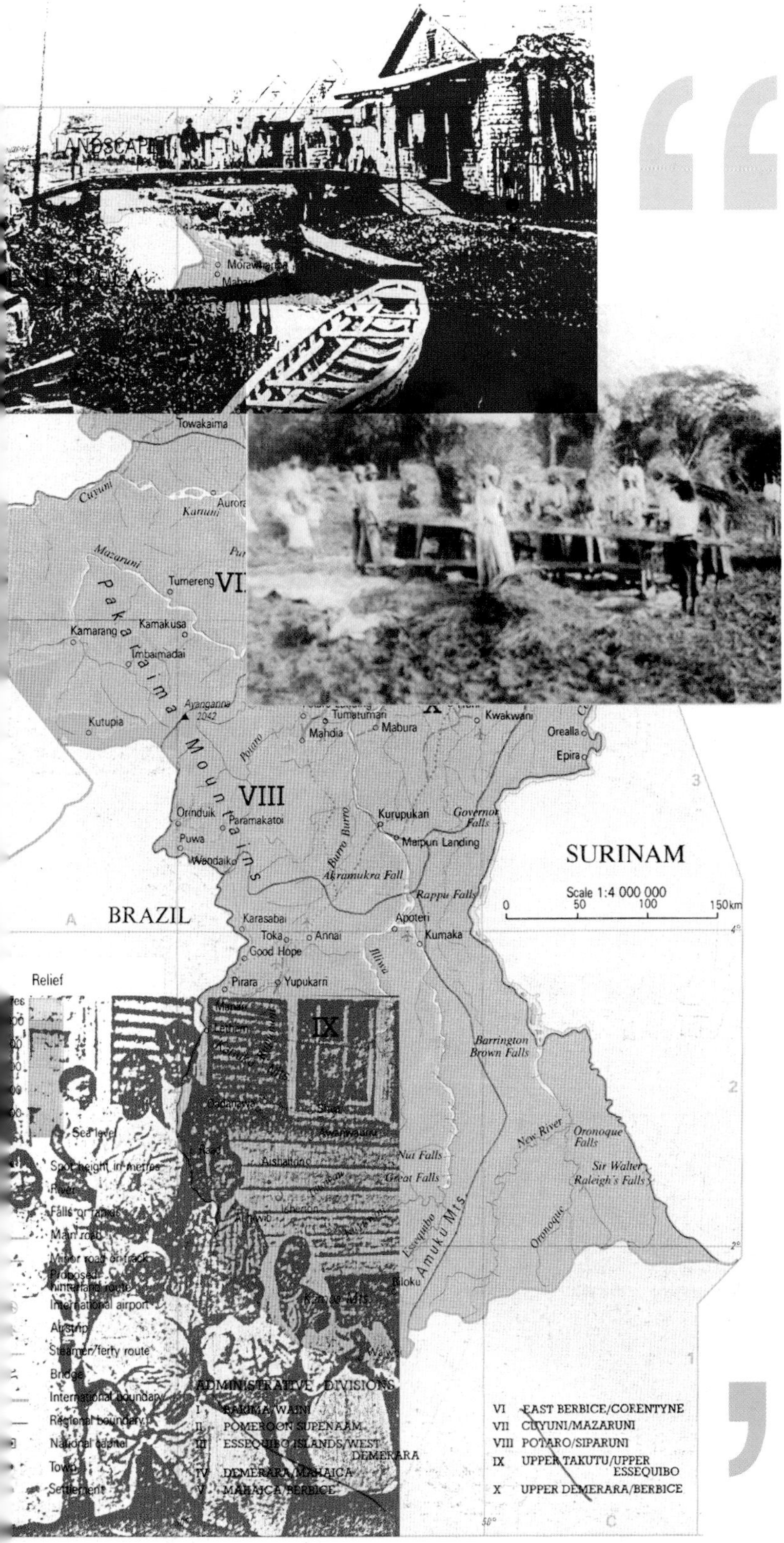

"These immigrants and their descendants have spread all over the country, reclaiming places formerly lying waste and opening up new tracts of land on the creeks and rivers from the Corentyne to the North-West district, with their thrifty, industrious habits, and unfaltering perseverance in the face of loss by drought and flood, they form the very "beau ideal" of settlers for a tropical country like this."

(J. Ruhomon, 160.)

"Tiger in the Stars"

"When he was a boy, an old man, it may have been his grandfather, used to tell him about the time he came across the 'black water' from India. It seemed like months, if not years, that voyage lasted. And the one clear memory the old man had was that each night on the deck he looked at the stars blazing in the sky and gradually picked out the shape of a tiger leaping in the sky amidst the constellations. That is what he recalled in the hardship and the monotony and the homesickness of the journey - a tiger leaping in the sky amid the stars. And he told it to his grandson and his grandson told it to me and during the Corentyne weekend traced himself for me that tiger-shape still blazing in the sky. And now at nights, at certain times of the year, I still look up and I think of the old man on his long voyage, and the generations who have done well after him, and it seems to me the tiger leaping in the stars must become for him a sort of symbol of pride and strength and beauty which he could not then hope to possess but which perhaps he could yearn for in his new land one day. And it seems to me, also, that the generations have not misplaced the symbol or the old man's yearning. Ian McDonald."

(Seecharan lx)

In 1838, the Whitby and Hesperus left Calcutta with 414 emigrants to work as indentured labourers on the plantations of British Guiana. This experiment with East Indian labour was severely criticized and emigration was suspended. In 1851, emigration was resumed and lasted until 1917. Efforts were made to solve immigration problems by the appointment of agents. James Crosby was the immigration agent from 1858--1880. During these years, he was a fearless champion of the rights and liberties of the Indian people.

"Women on the Canje Road" Adapted from a print by the wife of the manager of plantation Rose Hall, Guyana (19th Century)

Education

In British Guiana, the indentured labourers showed little interest in the education of their children. This was a common pattern throughout the Caribbean. The Canadian Presbyterian Church began its mission in British Guiana to convert the East Indians to Christianity.

As in Trinidad, the church established schools in several villages. By 1930, 34 primary schools were established and the Berbice High School and the Girls' High School provided secondary education. However, from 1920 the church encountered great difficulty in its conversion and education. There was a resurgence of Hinduism and the Hindu priests were preaching loyalty to the motherland and its customs.

In 1920, Indian children accounted for 24 per cent of the enrollment in primary schools. By 1935, this had increased to 36 per cent. The salaries of teachers in British Guiana were very low, and only seven per cent of all teachers were Indians, although 32 per cent were merchants and shopkeepers. The Indians' progress in education was well behind their progress in agriculture and commerce.

One of the reasons for this lack in education was the Sweltenham Circular of 1902 which stated that penalties should not be enforced for Indian children who did not attend school. In other words, education was not compulsory for Indian children as it was for others. Child labour was a part of life on the estates and the authorities did everything to continue this situation. However, at the end of the nineteen twenties, there was a small class of educated Indians, who stressed the importance of education and slowly the attitudes of parents began to change.

Since 1868, the Canadian Presbyterian Church had begun to work among the Indians in Trinidad. In 1885, the Rev John Gibson of the Presbyterian Church of Nova Scotia set up the first Canadian Mission for the Indians of British Guiana. In 1896, the Rev. J. B. Cropper arrived and worked in British Guaina for almost 50 years. He spoke fluent Hindi and used the language and culture of the Indians in teaching the Christian message. Bible stories were translated into Hindi, and 'Yeshu Kathas' were held at homes. These were based on the 'Hindu Kathas' when the stories of Ramayana were told in Hindu homes. In 1987, the first Canadian Mission school was founded at Helena. By 1918, there were 39 primary schools and one high school. But only about 2,000 East Indians were Presbyterians. Resistance to

Christianity was strong. The missionaries felt that since the Indians were isolated among strangers, they seemed to feel the need to vigorously preserve their national identity. By the nineteen-twenties, there was some prosperity in the Indian community and several beautiful temples and mosques were built in the colony. Large numbers in all the communities celebrated the Hindu and Muslim religious festivals.

Although the number of children attending primary school increased each year, many of these children did not stay in school beyond the age of 12. Only a few children who showed strong academic ability were allowed to complete primary education and in a few cases to proceed to secondary school. In September 1916, the Canadian Presbyterian Church opened the Berbice High School for Boys, and a few years later, in 1920, the Berbice High School for Girls opened its doors. The majority of Indians in British Guiana and Trinidad were educated in Presbyterian schools. The legacy of the Canadian Mission is an enduring one.

Settlers in British Guiana

In British Guiana, there was not the rapid movement off the estates as in Trinidad. Many Indians in British Guiana re-indentured themselves for a second five-year term on the estates in

Indian labourers at work in a sugar cane field.

the 1870s. By 1921, when all indentures were cancelled, about 40 per cent of the East Indians still resided on the estates.

The planters owned the best coastlands and there were many restrictions placed on the free Indians to prevent them from becoming landowners. Fertile land was not as easily available as in Trinidad. The planters needed labour and encouraged the Indians to remain on the estate, where they could be easily available. Portions of existing plantations were sold to Indians in small allotments for building a home and cultivation. The prolonged sugar depression, beginning in 1884, hastened the movement of the Indians off the estates. They acquired land in many ways. Most of them bought or rented private lands

An East Indian family group. The men and children wear western clothes, but the women wear traditional Indian clothing.

because this was the best land. Others accepted land grants instead of a return passage to India and some bought or leased non-plantation Crown lands. The Indians used these lands mainly for rice growing and cattle rearing. Some of the immigrants to British Guiana had been cattle herders or "ahirs" in India and they continued their tradition of rearing cattle. The cows were used for milk and the bullocks used in ploughing rice fields and treading out the paddy grains.

The planters discouraged the growth of the rice industry because the Indians would be independent and would not need to work in the sugar estates. By 1879, a small number of free Indians cultivated rice at Mahaica Ahary and Plantation Success. But the sugar depression changed the planters' attitude and Indian labour was shifted into rice cultivation. In 30 years from 1884--1914, the acres under rice cultivation increased from 2,000 to 47,000. British Guiana changed from being an importer of rice to an exporter. In 1916, more than one million dollars worth of rice was exported to mainly British, French and Dutch territories in the Caribbean. Other crops such as coffee, citrus and ground provisions were also grown on a smaller scale.

Threshing rice by hand

Movement into Towns

After indentureship, a few Indians moved into the towns. In 1891, 8 per cent of the population of Georgetown was Indian and by 1931, this had increased to 12 per cent. More Indians went to New Amsterdam where 14 per cent of the population was Indian in 1931. In the towns these Indians were employed as civil servants, teachers, court officers, grooms and gardeners. A few were businessmen operating dry goods stores and pharmacies. There were also a small number of doctors and lawyers. The merchants, professionals, large landlords, rice-millers and shopkeepers became the new elite among the

Indians in British Guiana. In 1916, they formed the British Guiana East Indian Association and tried to improve the conditions for their fellow Indians. Many of the Indians however, still lived in villages with poor housing and little education.

Cheddi Jagan describes the life of his parents

> *"Plantation life in British Guiana was hard. At a very early age, my parents had to join their mothers in the cane fields, my father at Albion and my mother at Port Mourant. They both worked in the creole gangs. My mother relates that she had to work from 7:00 am to 6:00 pm manuring sugar cane in the fields for eight cents per day, and also three times per week from midnight to 6:00 am fetching fine bagasse into the factory for four cents for the six-hour period. Her total take-home pay was about 60 cents per week. She often recalled how difficult those days were: "Bhaiya, ahwee proper punish" (brother we really suffered). My mother had the habit of*

calling me by the all-inclusive term "brother", a common practice among Indians.

. . . The plantation appeared to me as the hub of life. Everything revolved around sugar, and the sugar plantations seemed to own the world. They owned the cane fields and the factories; even the small pieces of land rented to some of the workers for family food production belonged to them. They owned the mansions occupied by the senior staff, and cottages owned by the dispensers, chemists, engineers, bookkeepers and drivers. They owned the logies (ranges) and huts where the labourers lived, the hospitals and every other important building. At one time they also owned and operated a rice-mill. Even the churches and schools came within their patronage and control.

. . . The plantation was indeed a world of its own. Or rather it was two worlds: the world of the exploiter and the world of the exploited: the world of the whites and the world of the non-whites. ”

(Jagan, 9 - 10)

BRITISH GUIANA: AVERAGE ANNUAL SUGAR PRODUCTION IN TONS

YEAR	SUGAR PRODUCED
1824-33	23,237
1824-33	55,936
1834-38	51,278
1839-46	31,875
1847-56	41,790
1857-66	61,284
1867-76	81,894
1877-86	88,728
1887-96	109,718
1897-1906	108,110
1907-1916	100,968

INDO-CARIBBEANS

Chapter 10

The world has always been in a state of movement and flux. I can think of no culture that is entirely of itself, self-generated. Africa has had movements all the time from Roman times; India - people crossed and recrossed: there is no one thing which is India: Europe: who can carry in his head all the movements of the people in Europe?
V.S. Naipaul.

(Jussawalla 164)

Three generations. The grandmother in this picture came from India, her son was born and lived in the Caribbean, and the grandson is now leaving on a journey to live in a new country.

When the Indians left India, they brought with them their holy books, and sandalwood incense, astrological charts, their food, their music and dance.

In the Caribbean they recreated an Indian way of life in their early villages. During their sojourn of 150 years in the Caribbean, a particular brand of Indianness was created. Although the temples, the mosques, the food and the names remain, these are becoming more Anglicized. In most homes, the language, which the immigrants brought has been lost. Indians in the Caribbean are English-speaking, and retain some words of Hindi for objects in the home and for religious rituals.

The caste system has broken down among Indians in the Caribbean, and social rank is now determined by education and earning power.

The custom of arranged marriages has almost ceased. Today, most young people prefer to choose their own marriage partners. The Indian household has changed from being an extended family, to a single family unit. In early days, young married couples lived with the husband's parents. Today, most young couples live with their parents for only a short period, and then set up their own household. In the New World, the immigrants were exposed to non-Indian cultural systems, and their own culture changed over time.

During the early days of indenture, Christianity and Western culture was the norm. This was the opinion held of the Indians:

Reverend Roy Neehall of the Presbyterian church in Trinidad wrote:

> *"On top of the physical hardship was the psychological effect of being regarded as the lowest of the low. There was a total lack of respect for their customs and religions, and little protection from those appointed to be their official protectors. They faced a callous and authoritarian colonial policy, a greedy plantocracy, and abject contempt, from many of his African folk who regarded them as interlopers and even scab labour"*
>
> (Indo-Caribbean resistance, 5)

During the post-independence era in the Caribbean, there has been a new movement to revive many Indian traditions.

Modern East Indian home

There is a renewed interest in the teachings and practices of Hinduism and Islam.

During 150 years of indentureship and settlement, the Indo-Caribbean community has struggled, endured and prospered in a new land.

Indo-Caribbeans have made a positive contribution to the economy of the countries where they have settled. Their close family ties, cultural and religious values help to foster thrift, hard work and savings.

After indentureship, many East Indians accepted land in lieu of a return passage to India. Their love for the land and work on the land, provided a base from which to acquire capital for further investment.

The following account is taken from the memoirs of a Muslim family, written by Wahid Ali

"After serving his indentureship, my grandfather (Khairat Ali/Cantally/Khairatee Meah) worked for some time as a labourer on the sugar-cane plantations, and then purchased land and became a farmer. His three sons grew up to join and strengthen his endeavours.

. . . Both my grandfather and father loved the land, and the harvest was produced with pride. Sugar cane was cultivated in the farm at Damp (Edinburgh). Cocoa, coffee and tonka beans were grown at the estate in Mamoral. Rice and other short crops were planted on the extensive acreage on which our home stood. My father had built pens in the backyard, his cows and mules spent the night in these. During the days, they had trees to graze on the land . . . My mother was the inspiration in the home. She took care of my ailing grandmother with devotion, she was the teacher and example in religious matters. Even before knowing the appropriate words, I sat by her side during the daily Salaat (prayers) . . . My mother had a burning desire for her children to receive a higher education (In celebration 58-59)"

Today, Indo-Caribbeans are members of the legal and medical professions. They have trained as accountants, pharmacists and engineers.

Some are members of the business community, many of them being involved in small business enterprises.

The hard work of their ancestors have led to a better life for them. However, there is still a portion of the Indo-Caribbean community who are victims of unemployment or underemployment. They suffer from poverty, malnutrition, low educational levels and poor housing. Opportunities must be created for this group and the disadvantaged classes of all ethnic groups.

The Indo-Caribbeans now constitute about a quarter of the English-speaking Caribbean, and is also represented in the population of the French and Dutch speaking countries. They have preserved ancient traditions, but have also created new traditions suitable for a new home in a new land.

As Indo-Caribbeans, they now belong to the Caribbean. They cherish the memories and the hopes their ancestors brought with them over the "kala-pani".

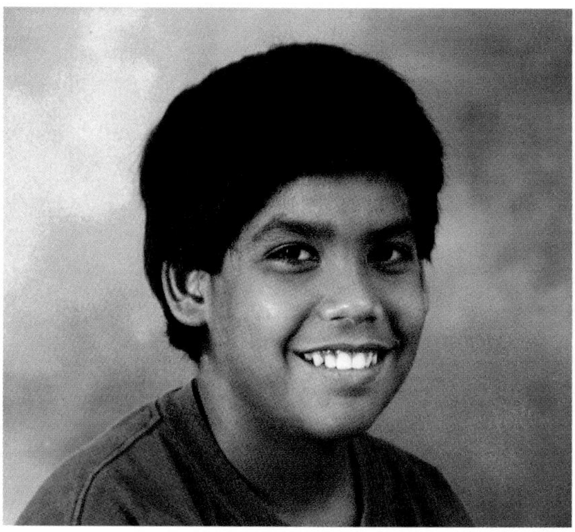

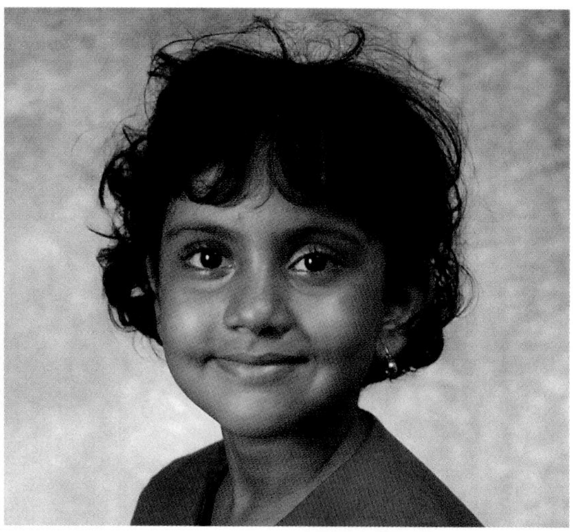

Names of some ships bringing East Indians to the West Indies

- Cheneb
- Dewa
- Elbe
- Ems
- Erne
- Fath al Rozack
- Firth
- Ganges
- Hereford
- India
- Indus
- Jumma
- Main
- Mutlah
- Pandora
- Rhone
- Shah Jehan
- Sheila
- Sutlej
- Virawa
- Volga

Jahagibahin – Shipsister

Appendix A

Hall of Fame

***Cheddi Jagan* (1918 – 1997)** *was born in Port Morant, Coventyre Guyana. He founded the People's Progressive Party in 1950. After a long political struggle, he became President of Guyana in October 1992. He was an outstanding political figure in Guyana and the Caribbean, and was a champion of the working class.*

His writings include

Forbidden freedom: the story of British Guiana. 3rd ed. London: Hansib, 1994

Rooting for labour. Guyana (s.n., 1993).

The West on trial. My fight for Guyana's freedom. Berlin: Seven Seas Publishers, 1972.

Collection of Speeches and writings

- *Selected Speeches 1992 – 1994*
- *A New Global Human Order: speeches and writings 1993 – 1996*
- *Steps toward Caribbean unity. Georgetown, Guyana: People's Progressive Party, 1989.*

Sonny Ramadhin, 1929 *– was the first East Indian to play on the West Indian cricket team. He was a spin bowler, and the youngest member of the team to tour England in 1949 – 50.*

Together with the Jamaican bowler, Alfred Valentine, they made cricket history with the following scores; Ramadhin 5 wickets for 66 runs; Valentine 4 wickets for 43 runs. Ramadhin took the most wickets – 135 for the best average 14.58, during this tour.

A calypso was composed in their honour by Lord Kitchener from Trinidad.

"Yardley (the English captain) tried his best,

But Goddard (the West Indian captain) won the test

With those two pals of mine

Ramadhin and Valentine"

Samuel Dickson Selvon (1923 – 1997) *has written ten novels, one collection of short stories, and numerous articles. His awards include two Guggenheim fellowships, and a Trinidad and Tobago Hummingbird medal.*

He describes growing up in Trinidad ***"By the time I was in my teens, I was a product of my environment, as Trinidadian as anyone could claim to be, quite at ease with the cosmopolitan attitude, and I had no desire to isolate myself from the mixture of races that comprised the community."*** (*Trinidad Express,* 23 Sept. 1979)

His writings include

A brighter sun. London: Longman, 1979.

An island is a world. London: Wingate, 1955.

The lonely Londoners. Toronto: TSAR, 1991.

Turn again tiger. New York: St. Martin's Press, 1959.

Ways of sunlight. Harlow, Essex: Longman. 1985.

Appendix B

EAST INDIAN MIGRANTS TO THE BRITISH CARIBBEAN, BY COUNTRY OF ARRIVAL, 1838–1918

Country	India (1838 - 1918)
British Guiana	238,909
Trinidad	143,939
Jamaica	36,412
Grenada	3,200
St. Vincent	2,472
St. Lucia	4,354
St. Kitts	337
Antigua	–
British Honduras	–
Dominica	–
Total	**429,632**

Source: George Roberts and Joycelyn Byrne, "Summary Statistics on Indenture and Associated Migration Affecting the West Indies, 1834 -1918." *Population Studies* 20,1 (1966) p.127

EAST INDIAN MIGRANTS TO THE BRITISH CARIBBEAN, BY YEAR OF ARRIVAL, 1838–1918

Year	East Indian Migrants
1838	396
1845 -50	22,493
1851-55	15,035
1856-60	31,954
1861-65	28,187
1866-70	40,965
1871-75	42,635
1876-80	44,305
1881-85	34,114
1886-90	23,470
1901-1905	27,081
1906-1910	26,094
1911-1915	14,446
1916-1918	4,531
TOTAL	**429,623**

Source: George Roberts and Joycelyn Byrne, "Summary Statistics on Indenture and Associated Migration Affecting the West Indies, 1834-1918." *Population Studies* 20,1 (1966) p.129

Appendix C

HINDU NAMES AND MEANINGS

Name	Sex	Meaning
Aditi	Female	Free and unbounded
Ajay	Male	God
Ambar	Female	Sky
Ambika	Female	Goddess of destruction
Ananda	Female	Bliss
Aruna	Female	Radiance
Baka	Female	Crane
Bali	Male	Mighty Warrior
Balin	Male	Mighty Warrior
Bel	Female	Sacred Wood Apple tree
Chander	Male	Moon
Darshan	Male	A Hindu God
Devi	Female	Resides in Heaven
Ganesa	Female	Good Luck
Hastin	Male	Elephant
Hinda	Female	Female Deer
Indira	Female	India
Indra	Male	God of Power
Jafar	Male	Little Stream
Jaya	Unisex	Name of God; Victory
Jayne	Female	Victorious
Jivin	Male	To give Life
Kala	Female	Time; Black
Kalkin	Male	Tenth incarnation of God Vishnu
Kamal	Male	Name of a god
Kamala	Female	Lotus
Kanya	female	Virgin
Karma	Female	Fate
Kasi	Female	From the holy city
Kaveri	Female	Sacred River of India
Kavindra	Female	Mighty Poet
Kedar	Male	Mountain Lord; Powerful

Name	Sex	Meaning
Kinton	Male	Crowned
Kiran	Female	Ray
Lal	Male	Beloved
Lalasa	Female	Love
Latika	Female	Elegant
Linu	Male	Lily
Mahesa	Male	Great Lord
Mandara	Female	Mythical Tree
Matrika	Female	Mother; Name of a goddess
Maya	Female	Divine creative force in everything
Mayon		The black God
Mela		Religious Gathering
Mesha	Male	Ram; Born under sign of Aries
Narmanda		Name of a river
Natesa		Dance Lord
Nitara		Deeply rooted
Nitaka		Angel of precious stones
Pandita		Scholar
Ramya	Female	Beautiful; Elegant
Rani	Female	A queen
Ratri		Night
Ravi	Male	Benevolent, sun god
Rohana	Female	Sandalwood
Sagara		Ocean
Sahen		Falcon
Sakti		Energy; Goddess
Sandya		Sunset time; Name of a god
Sarisha		Charming
Sarngin		Name of God Vishnu
Sarojin		Lotus Like
Sesha		Serpent who symbolizes time
Shanata	Female	Peaceful
Shantha		Peace; Name of a God
Shashi		Moonbeam
Thaman		Name of a God
Veda	Female	Sacred Knowledge
Vrinda		Divine virtue and strength

ARABIC NAMES AND MEANINGS

Name	Sex	Meaning
Abdel	Male	Servant
Adiva	Female	Pleasant, gentle
Ainin	Female	Precious, eye
Akil		Intelligent, thoughtful
Akilah		Intelligent, logical
Aleser		Lion
Ali	Male	Form of ALISON - noble, kind
Alia		Loftiness
Alim		Wise, learned
Alima	Female	Wise
Alzena	Female	The woman
Amber	Female	Reddish-yellow precious jewel
Ameerah	Female	Princess
Anisa	Female	Friendly
Atifa		Affection
Ayisha		Living
Banan		Fingertips
Barakah		White one
Basil	Male	Brave
Basimah		Smiling
Bethany	Female	Daughter of the Lord
Bilal	Male	First convert of Muhammad
Burhan		Proof
Cala		Castle
Cantara		Small bridge
Carna	Female	Horn
Cemal	Female	Beauty
Coman		Noble
Fatima	Female	Daughter of Muhammad
Fatin		Captivating
Ferran	Male	Baker
Ginton		A garden

Name	Sex	Meaning
Givon	Male	Hill, High Place
Hadi		Guide to righteousness, gift
Hadiya		Guide to righteousness, gift
Hamal	Male	Lamb
Hanan		Mercy
Hasna	Female	Beautiful
Hassan	Male	Handsome
Iman		Faith, belief
Jabir		Comforter
Jala	Female	Charity
Jaleel		Great, fine
Jamal	Male	Beauty
Jamilah		Beautiful
Jed	Male	The hand
Jibril		Archangel Gabriel
Kadin		Friend, companion
Kalil	Male	Good friend
Kalila	Female	Beloved
Kamilah	Female	The perfect one
Kardal		Mustard seed
Kareem	Male	Noble, Exalted
Karida	Female	Untouched, virginal
Kateb		Writer
Khalidah		Immortal
Khalil	Male	Friend
Khoury		Priest
Lasca	Female	Army or Soldier
Leila	Female	Born at night, black
Leron		The song is mine
Lila	Female	Night
Lina	Female	Tender
Malik	Male	Master
Mansur		Divinely aided
Martha	Female	A lady

Name	**Sex**	**Meaning**
Matana		Gift
Muhammad	Male	Praised
Naimah		Living a soft, enjoyable life
Nazirah		Equal, like
Nimah		Blessing, loan
Nuri	Male	Fire
Omar	Male	First born son
Qamra		Moon
Reyhan		Favoured by god
Rihana	Female	Sweet basil
Rimon	Male	Pomegranate
Sabirah		Patient
Sabra	Female	Thorny cactus
Sadira	Female	Ostrich returning from water
Sahara	Female	The Moon
Sakinah		God-inspired peace-of-mind, tranquillity
Salimah		Safe, healthy
Samien		To be heard
Samirah		Entertaining companion
Sammon		Grocer
Sarea		Name of an angel
Saree	Female	Most noble
Seif		Sword of religion
Selima	Female	Peace

Name	Sex	Meaning
Shakira	Female	Grateful
Shammara	Male	He girded his loins
Shunnar		Pleasant
Siham		Arrows
Tabitha	Female	A gazelle
Tahirah	Female	Chaste, pure
Thana		Gratitude
Thara		Wealth
Vega	Female	Falling Star
Wijdan		Ecstasy
Xavier	Male	Bright
Xaviera	Female	Brilliant
Yasmin	Female	Jasmine
Zahirah		Shining, luminous
Zahra		White
Zaida	Female	Fortunate One
Zara	Female	Form of SARA
Zarifa	Female	Moves with Grace
Zaza	Female	Flowery
Zeke	Male	The memory of the lord
Zoltan	Male	Sultan, Ruler
Zuleika	Female	The fair one
Zulema	Female	Peace

Glossary

Names	Meanings
Aloo	Irish potato
Amchar	Mango pickle
Adrak	Ginger
Arkati	Recruiter
Babu	Old man
Baigan	Eggplant
Bap	Father
Bhajan	Hymn
Bhagi	Spinach
Bhai	Brother
Bhat	Boiled rice
Bilna	Rolling pin
Dahi	Yogurt
Dahl	Split peas
Bodi/bora	Long bean
Channa	Chick peas
Chulha	Earthen fireplace, used for cooking
Dantal	Metal rods for making music
Dhanai	Coriander
Dholak	Drum
Dhoti	Loin cloth
Ghee	Clarified butter
Geera	Cumin
Gainda	Marigold
Gondana	Tattoo
Haldi	Tumeric
Jata	Stone mill for making flour
Jahajibhai	Shipbrother
Jahajibahin	Shipsister
Kala pani	Black water
Kali mirch	Black pepper
Kajat	Caste
Kumhar	Potter
Khir	Rice pudding
Lathi	Stick
Lota	Water jug
Murai	Radish
Neemac	Salt
Phool	Flower
Pundit	Hindu priest
Sem	Flat bean
Silanti	Grinding store for spice
Sindoor	Vermillion used in the parting of hair
Roti	Quick bread in the shape of flat pancakes
Sitar	Stringed musical instrument
Tabla	Drum
Tarkari	Cooked vegetables

Bibliography

- **Angel, W. H.** A return to the middle passage: the Clipper ship Sheila. Port of Spain: Caribbean Information Systems, 1995.

- **Beckles, Hilary**. White servitude and black slavery in Barbados, 1627-1715. Knoxville: University of Tenessee Press, 1989.

- **Bedaridé, François**. The social responsibility of the historian. Providence, R. I., Bergham Books, 1994.

- **Birbalsingh, Frank** (ed). **Jahagi bhai**: an anthology of Indo-Caribbean literature. Toronto: TSAR, 1993.

  _______ . Indo-Caribbean resistance. Toronto: TSAR, 1993.

- **Bisnauth, Dale**. "The East Indian immigrant society in British Guiana, 1891--1930." Ph.D thesis. University of the West Indies, Mona, Jamaica, 1977.

- *Caribbean Quarterly*. Vol. 26, 2000.

- **Dabydeen, David** and **Brinsley Samaroo** (eds). India in the Caribbean. London : Hansib, 1987.

- **Das, Mahadai.** Bones. Leeds: Peepal Tree Press, 1988.

- **Hamid, Idris**. Troubling of the waters. San Fernando, Trinidad: Rahaman Printery, 1973.

- **Jagan, Cheddi.** My fight for Guyana's Freedom. Milton, Ont.: Harpy, 1998.

- **Jussawalla, Feroza**, ed. Conversations with V.S. Naipaul. Jackson: University Press of Mississippi, 1997.

- **La Guerre, John,** ed. From Calcutta to Caroni: the East Indians of Trinidad. Port-of-Spain: Longman, 1974.

- **Look Lai, Walton**. Indentured Labour, Caribbean sugar. Baltimore: Johns Hopkins Press, 1993.

- **Lubbock, Basil**. Coolie ships and oil sailors. Glasgow: Brown, Son & Ferguson, 1935.

- **Mahabir, Noor Kumar.** Still cry. New York: Callaloux, 1985.

- **Mansingh, Laxmi and Ajai Mansingh**. Home away from home: 150 years of Indian presence in Jamaica. Kingston: Ian Randle Publishers, 1999.

- **Morton, John**. Diary. Toronto: s.n., 1916.

- **Naipaul, V.S**. The enigma of arrival. New York: Knopf, 1987.

- **______.** India: a million mutinies now. London: Heinemann, 1990.

- **Nehru, Jawaharlal.** The discovery of India. Garden City: Doubleday, 1960.

- **Ramesar, Marianne**. Survivors of another crossing. St Augustine, Trinidad: U.W.I. School of Continuing Studies, 1994.

- **Ruhomon, Peter**. Centenary history of the East Indians in British Guiana, 1898-1938. Georgetown: Daily Chronicle, 1947.

- **Samaroo, Brinsley** (ed). In celebration of 150 years of Indian contribution to Trinidad & Tobago. Port of Spain: Historical Publications, 1995.

- **Seecharan, Clem**. 'Tiger in the stars' : the anatomy of Indian achievement in British Guiana, 1919-1929. London: Macmillan, 1997.

- **Shepherd, Verene**. Transients to settlers: the experience of Indians in Jamaica 1854-1950. Leeds: Peepal Tree Press, 1994.

- **Singh, Kelvin**. Blood-stained tombs: the Muharram massacre. Basingstoke: Macmillan Caribbean, 1988.

- **Tagore, Rabindranath.** Gitanjali: the song offerings. New Delhi: Macmillan, 1980.

- **Tinker, Hugh.** A new system of slavery. London: Hansib, 1999.

- **World Book Encyclopedia**. London: World Book Inc. 1992.

Index